Is
Religion
Dangerous?

Is Religion Dangerous?

KEITH WARD

William B. Eerdmans Publishing Company

Grand Rapids, Michigan / Cambridge, U.K.

First published 2006 in the United Kingdom by
Lion Hudson plc
Mayfield House, 256 Banbury Road,
Oxford OX2 7DH, England

This edition published 2007 in the United States of America by
Wm. B. Eerdmans Publishing Co.
2140 Oak Industrial Drive N.E., Grand Rapids, Michigan 49505 /
P.O. Box 163, Cambridge CB3 9PU U.K.
www.eerdmans.com

Printed in the United States of America

12 11 10 09 08 07   7 6 5 4 3 2 1

Library of Congress Cataloging-in-Publication Data

ISBN 978-0-8028-4508-5

Acknowledgments

pp. 32, 101, 102, 114, 119 Scripture quotations are taken from the New Revised
Standard Version published by HarperCollins Publishers, copyright © 1989 by
the Division of Christian Education of the National Council of the Churches of
Christ in the USA, and are used by permission. All rights reserved.

Contents

8344

Introduction: What is religion?

The question at issue

Is religion dangerous? Does it do more harm than good? Is it a force for evil, even 'the root of all evil' — the title of a short British television series presented by Professor Richard Dawkins? Is it something of which we should be afraid, something we should oppose because it corrupts the minds of children and leads to terrorism and violence, as Polly Toynbee has asserted in the *Guardian* newspaper (an excellent quality British paper that seems to have an obsessive antipathy to religion)?

I will come clean at once — I think such assertions are absurd. Worse than that, they ignore the available evidence from history, from psychology and sociology, and from philosophy. They refuse to investigate the question in a properly rigorous way, and substitute rhetoric for analysis. Oddly enough, that is just what they tend to accuse religious believers of doing. There is something there, I think, that needs to be explained.

In this book, however, I will not try to psychoanalyse the denigrators of religion. I will focus on the main question at issue: does religion do more harm than good? I will look at the evidence that is available from history, sociology and psychology. My conclusion will be that religion does some harm and some good, but most people, faced with the evidence, will probably agree that it does a great deal more good than harm, and that we would be much worse off as a species without any religion. I will go further, and say that it is very important that there should be some religion about, if humans are to have a hopeful future. Of course not all religions are the same. It is quite important what sort of religion we choose, and of course we should choose the religion with the highest intellectual and moral standards that we can find. But I will on the whole let the evidence speak for itself, and will refrain from too much propaganda.

What is religion anyway?

I have to begin by pointing out that the question already contains two extremely contentious terms – 'religion' and 'dangerous'. If you go to college and take a course on 'religion', probably the first thing you will be told is that there is no such thing as 'religion'. Of course, there are many religions, but they are very different from one another. And there are many belief-systems that might deny they are religions. Is Communism a religion? Or football? Or Scientology? How do we know what a religion is?

When I was Professor of the History and Philosophy of Religion at London University, I was consulted by a senior British lawyer who asked me to provide a definition of 'religion'. The reason was that in British law if you are a religion you can claim exemption from tax. It seems that all sorts of social clubs, some of which met in the front rooms of semi-detached houses in Wapping, were claiming to be religions in order to get those benefits, and the authorities wanted some way of telling what was a religion and what was not.

I confess that I was unable to come up with a definition, or at least with a definition that would satisfy a lawyer. You could say, as the Shorter Oxford English Dictionary does, that religion is 'belief in or sensing of some superhuman controlling power or powers, entitled to obedience, reverence and worship, or in a system defining a code of living, especially as a means to achieve spiritual or material improvement'. When you get a definition as long as that, you know you are in trouble. The first half of the definition, 'belief in some superhuman controlling power', could well apply to belief in some superhuman alien from the planet Krypton, perhaps to Superman himself. I suspect that is what some atheists think religion is. The second half, however, 'a system defining a code of living as a means to achieve improvement', could apply to the Constitution of the Labour Party. It sounds as though the ideal religion would be one that combined membership of the Labour Party with a strong belief in the existence of Superman.

The problem is that if you have a short, snappy definition (such as the early anthropologist E. B. Tylor's minimum definition of religion as 'belief in spiritual beings'), you eliminate things like Buddhism, which are pretty obviously religions. But if you have a long, vague definition (such as 'belief in a code of living to achieve improvement...') you will find it hard to eliminate anything at all, including attendance at university extra-mural classes.

If you do not know what 'religion' is, you can hardly decide whether it is dangerous or not. Perhaps you do not like the Labour Party, but you love Superman. The danger is that you might just pick all the things you do not like, and call them 'religion'. Then people who disagree with you could pick all the things they liked and call them 'religion'. The debate would go nowhere, because the basic terms are not agreed.

There are obviously many different sorts of things that we can call 'religion'. Since religions have existed as far back as we can trace the history of the human race, and in almost every society we know about, there are going to be as many different religions as there are human cultures. They are going to exhibit all the variety and all the various stages of development of the cultures in which they exist. That is going to make it virtually impossible to say that religion, as such, at every stage of its development and in all its varieties, is dangerous. Unless, that is, you are prepared to say that human culture as such is dangerous, or even that human life itself is dangerous. In a sense, of course, it is. Human life is, as we all know, ultimately fatal. And all human cultures are morally deficient, they can easily become tyrannical and oppressive, and each of them is considered dangerous by somebody else.

That is not a very helpful statement, and it fails to throw any light on what the real dangers to human life are, and on how we might best avoid them. Nevertheless there is a very important negative point here. If human societies have developed, and have taken many different forms, often in strong disagreement with one another, then their religions will also be subject to development and diversity.

The study of early religion

One rhetorical tactic of those who oppose religion is to take its most primitive or undeveloped forms and consider them as definitive of religion. This was the tactic of many early anthropologists such as Edward Tylor, Sir James Frazer and Emile Durkheim, in the late nineteenth and early twentieth centuries, who argued that the essence of religion could be discovered by examining its most 'primitive' forms. Despite the fact that there is virtually no extant evidence for what the origins of religion were (since the origins must have been hundreds of thousands of years ago), this has not stopped scholars making definitive claims about what really happened. This is an instance in which claims to certainty are in inverse proportion to the amount of evidence available.

The result of all this scholarly fantasizing was that

religion turned out, amazingly, to be a very primitive phenomenon that could now be seen to be superstitious, and had long been superseded by science (or, in Durkheim's case, by social theory).

In his definitive work, *Theories of Primitive Religion*[1], the Oxford anthropologist Evans-Pritchard has established the uselessness of all this fantasizing, which is based on unreliable, uncritical or non-existent evidence.

Unfortunately some writers have not yet realised this. Thus Daniel Dennett, in his recent book *Breaking the Spell*[2], challenges scholars to 'break the spell' that stops us from investigating religion scientifically, and to set out on a fully critical study of religion. He does not seem to realise that the spell was broken as long ago as 1884, when E. B. Tylor was appointed to a Readership in Anthropology at Oxford University. Tylor and Sir James Frazer, author of *The Golden Bough*[3], both set out to study the phenomenon of religion from a strictly scientific (that is, anthropological) point of view. Both of them regarded religious belief as outmoded superstition, and so they perfectly fitted Dennett's requirement that a scientific study of religion should treat it as a 'purely natural' phenomenon.

Anthropology was then in its infancy, and more recent and sophisticated anthropologists of religion look with a great deal of scepticism on this proposal. The trouble with it is that it sets out with the assumption that all religious beliefs (all the ones about non-natural or non-physical realities like God) are false or irrelevant. That is hardly a dispassionate view, and it is not likely to evoke much sympathy for religious beliefs. It amounts to treating all religious believers as deluded or perhaps even as mentally challenged.

Most contemporary anthropologists think that beginning with such a strong prejudice is not the right way to undertake a properly scientific enquiry. We need to pay much more attention to what people say about their own

beliefs, and the reasons they themselves give for holding
them.

However, such an attempt at neutrality about questions
of truth was not part of Tylor and Frazer's programme.
They assumed religious beliefs were false, and so they had
not to explain them, but to explain them away. Their
argument was fairly simple. Religion originated in the early
pre-history of humanity. People then were very simple and
superstitious. So religious beliefs are hangovers from a
simple and superstitious age. If they had known about
evolutionary psychology, they would probably have said that
religious beliefs were conducive to evolutionary fitness
then, and have been genetically programmed into us. But
they are no longer conducive to survival, and we can see that
they are quite irrational. They have in fact been wholly
replaced by properly scientific beliefs by anyone who has
any sense.

Unfortunately this simple argument is wholly mistaken,
and is hardly taken seriously by any contemporary
anthropologist. It depends on two major errors – that the
true nature of religion is given by its earliest examples, and
that we know what the religious beliefs of the earliest
humans were like.

Thus Dennett does not hesitate to tell us that early
humans took their religious beliefs literally. They really
thought that there were invisible persons who moved the
clouds around and made it rain. Presumably Dennett has
some magical way of accessing the minds of humans who
lived tens or even hundreds of thousands of years ago. Most
of us realise that there is no possible way of knowing what
such pre-hominids thought. He also tells us that the
earliest form of religious belief was animism: the natural if
childlike delusion that everything in the world – trees,
clouds and rivers – has intentions and feelings. This
developed into theism, basically because one all-powerful
God can give a better pay-off than many conflicting spirits.

Well, maybe so. But is Dennett's statement a scientific one? Can it ever be verified or falsified? It seems more like pure speculation without any evidence at all – a story that might appeal to us, given certain general beliefs about the universe and a generally materialist philosophical outlook.

Taking things literally

It may in fact be quite misleading to think that early believers used to take things quite literally, and that metaphor is some later and more sophisticated ploy. What evidence do we have that the first religious believers, living perhaps hundreds of thousands of years ago, before anything was written down, were literalists about God? None at all. Of course, we have no evidence that they were not literalists either. We simply have no way of knowing how they interpreted their religious ideas. The truth is that we know virtually nothing about the first origins of religious belief.

From a purely scientific point of view, all we have to go on are grave-goods and archaeological remains. We might also examine some present-day technologically undeveloped tribes, whom we might think are more like early humans than technologically sophisticated people are. Or we might look at child development, on the assumption that humans have evolved from a more childlike way of thinking over many aeons. But archaeological remains do not tell us how they were interpreted.

For example, what does the statue of the *Willendorf Venus* (dated to around 20,000 BCE) represent? Is it a primitive *Playboy* centrefold? Did anybody ever think it represented some real portly goddess, who lived on a mountain somewhere? Is it a symbolic expression of fertility that does not represent any particular object, but symbolises some powerful psychological force? We do not, and will never, know.

If we look at present-day societies that use images of gods (in India, for example), anthropologists find that worshippers are in general puzzled by the question, 'Do you think these gods are real?' It looks as if the question of literalism simply has not arisen. That is how the gods are represented, and people are aware that traditions of representation have developed over time.

It is a bit like asking a modern Christian who has a picture of Jesus on the wall, 'Do you think Jesus really looked like that?' Of course, some people would say yes, largely because they do not want to say no! But most realise that we have no idea of what Jesus looked like. It is just that some images have become rooted in Christian imagination. If they are reasonably sophisticated, such images may be useful aids to devotion, enabling Christians to form a picture that can be used for meditation, perhaps. But it would be wrong to take them as literal representations, like photographs. In other words, if taken too literally they are actually misleading. If they lead us to think that Jesus was a white American male, as some popular pictures do, they are definitely misleading, since he was a Middle Eastern Semite (that is, probably more like an Arab). So the sophisticated worshipper may use an image, but will know that we must be prepared to move beyond the image.

If we now think about ancient humans, are we seriously to believe that they all thought there really were fat ladies living in some distant forest, who might help them to have more babies? Or are we asked to accept that tribal societies in the world today, living hundreds of thousands of years later than early humans, are a good guide to what early humans believed?

There used to be a fashion – in Emile Durkheim, for instance – for thinking that Australian Aborigines were nearest to early humans, since their technology was very undeveloped. It turns out that most of Durkheim's information about Aboriginal religion (based on the early work of the anthropologists Spenser and Gillen) was incorrect, and Aboriginal Australians with degrees in sociology can now provide much more sophisticated accounts of Aboriginal religion. For a start, Aboriginal religious art is full of symbolism, and is not literal at all. But the real question is: on what evidence does anyone think that humans have moved from literal to symbolic interpretations?

If humans have evolved, then it will be true that at some stage, many tens of thousands of years ago, human thought would have been less developed than it is now. But does that mean it would have been more literal? Perhaps literalness is a late development, and the idea that artefacts should literally be like what they represent – or even the idea of 'literalness' itself – is a concept that only developed when humans began to think scientifically or analytically.

It could be that the obsession with 'literal truth' is itself a product of the scientific outlook, and of the belief that only literal truths are true at all. In psychiatry, over-literalness and the inability to understand metaphor is often a symptom of psychotic illness. Yet even in science we have to learn to work with metaphors, as when we say that electricity 'flows' along wires, or that electrons are probability 'waves' in Hilbert space (if we ever do say that sort of thing). Metaphor is essential to thinking, especially about the complexities of human personality and feeling. Metaphorical thinking is deeply rooted in the human mind. It may be the case that very early human thinking was more metaphorical than literal in nature.

The development of religious ideas

If we look at the way children develop, it seems that at an early age they live in a highly imaginative fantasy world, in which drawers can contain monsters and broomsticks can be fairy wands, and the realistic causal connections adults make are overlaid by magical connections. The child's world is hardly literal. It is a world of 'magic realism' in which fact and fantasy, imagination and observation, are closely intertwined.

In such a world, internal feelings and moods can easily be projected onto the external world, though not in any systematic way. It would seem to be wholly anachronistic to call childhood beliefs 'literal'. Rather, in that world fact and fantasy are hard to separate, and imagined realities are as real as observed facts.

At this point the atheist might cheer up and say, 'All right, young children are not literalists. But they do project their fantasies onto the external world. And that is just what God is – a projected fantasy.'

In my view, religious believers should to some extent accept this. Ideas of God *are* imaginative projections. An idea of God (remember, I am talking about *our idea* of God, not about God!) is a construct of the imagination, not a perceived object in the external world. It is a construct because it is trying to form some image of a reality that is beyond all images. The only question is whether it is a construct that has no basis in reality, or whether it is striving to depict some sort of objective reality.

Think for a moment of mathematics. That is certainly a construct of the human imagination. In fact it takes a very high degree of imagination to be a good mathematician. Yet a good many mathematicians believe that they are not just inventing mathematics. They are discovering a set of objective truths – but they are discovering it by using their imaginations as creatively as possible. Intellectual imagination may be a means of access to a reality that cannot be known by the senses. For many mathematicians it is precisely that.

So in religion there may be an appropriate form of intellectual imagination that gives access to a reality that cannot be known by the senses. Of course many of the nineteenth-century scientific investigators of religion did not believe that there was any such 'suprasensory' reality. As good basically Humean empiricists, they thought that all proper human knowledge had to be based on and confined to objects of sense – experience. This rules out God and spiritual reality by definition. Many of us think that it rules out mathematics, quantum physics, objective moral truths, and a great deal else too – perhaps it even rules out other people, as subjects of consciousness. Anyway, these investigators, not because of science but because of their basic philosophical outlook, regarded religion as based on an illusion, as a fantasy.

Given that religious belief was based on illusion, they then had to explain how the illusion arose. One popular theory of the origin of religion was the causal theory: early humans invented God to explain why things happen, why thunder and lightning occur or why plants grow in the Spring. Religion is a sort of very primitive science.

But if we look at present religious beliefs, they are not only, or even mainly, used to explain why things happen. They are used to console, inspire and motivate, but not to explain. As early non-religious anthropologists were quick to point out, explanations in terms of the gods do not really explain anything. For we never know what the gods might do next. So, even today, to explain why something like the Indian Ocean tsunami happened by saying that God willed it just leaves us with the mystery of why God should have willed it. The explanation is more mysterious than the event itself. It is not really any explanation at all.

It looks as if the roots of religious belief do not lie in attempts to explain why things happen. If we ask intelligent modern believers where the roots of their belief lie, many different sorts of answers would be given, but rarely that their beliefs explain why things happen. One answer, and I think it is a very important one, would refer to experiences of a transcendent power and value, of greater significance and moral power than anything human. The metaphors of religious speech — metaphors of 'dazzling darkness' or 'personal presence' — are inadequate attempts to express such experiences of transcendence. Why should it ever have been different? For all we know, early religion could have originated in experiences of a transcendent spiritual reality, especially in the vivid experiences, sometimes in dreams and visions, of shamans or holy men and women.

Such experiences could, of course, be illusory. The scientific investigator of religion must take that possibility seriously. But the possibility that they are not illusory must also be taken seriously. Suppose that there is a transcendent suprasensory reality, such as God. Only the mind could give access to it, and imagination, carefully controlled by reason, might be an important element of mental creativity. If you also suppose that the supreme spiritual reality is personal in character, you might expect that it would take an active role in helping to shape and guide the imagination. It might not simply override imagination, but interact with it to develop greater insight into its nature.

So we might see the development of early religion as the shaping of rational imagination towards a more intellectually structured and morally developed idea of spiritual reality. This is the sort of thing a religious believer who accepts the evolutionary development of religions would expect. It is consistent with such evidence as we have. It is certainly as reasonable a view as the speculation that humans began as literalists who later had to withdraw many of their literalist claims. If there is a God, it is actually a much more reasonable view. At the very least, the dispassionate study of religion should be open to both these views. Insofar as a serious concern for truth exists, this is not a place for misrepresenting, mocking or trivialising the beliefs of others.

Religions as diverse and developing

The important thing to see is that all speculations about the origins of religion are very poorly evidenced, and depend almost entirely on our present attitudes towards religious belief — on whether we think it is reasonable or fundamentally a delusion. Study of the origins of religion cannot help in making that decision, since the results of such a study will already incorporate our views about the authenticity and truth of present religion.

Yet, although nineteenth-century naturalistic approaches to religion would not be taken seriously by anthropologists today, they were not completely useless. They began the modern approach to religion as a global phenomenon that could be studied from a scientific viewpoint — even though they did not manage the 'scientific' bit very well, by modern standards. And their approach represented the first serious acceptance of an evolutionary perspective, the realisation that religious beliefs and practices must have evolved from earlier, less sophisticated forms, and that these forms might well leave their imprint on modern minds in partly unperceived ways.

While it would be wise to be agnostic about exactly what these early forms were, we have to allow for a growing rationalisation and moralisation of religion, just as we do in the natural sciences. There can be no serious doubt that rational and moral insight has grown since the earliest hominids walked the earth.

In science, we may greatly admire the work of Aristotle, but we realise that most of the things he said about physics were mistaken. We know that Isaac Newton devoted much time to the study of alchemy, but that it was a false trail that led nowhere. Since the sixteenth century, our scientific views of the world have changed considerably. It would be a mad anthropologist who said that the essence of science is to be found in its earliest origins, and that

Aristotle and alchemy define what science really is.

So in religion we would expect that its earliest discernible beginnings (and the Hebrew Bible is one of the most interesting records of one form of early religion and its development) would be precisely that – early beginnings of something that developed considerably. If we find in the Bible (as we do) that God used to be thought of as one among many gods, and that the prophets used to be called 'seers' or fortune-tellers, that should not lead us to say that these are the really essential Jewish or Christian beliefs. They are the beginnings of the faith of Israel, which was reformed by Moses, then by the great prophets of the eighth and sixth centuries BCE, and then – for Christians – by Jesus.

We are able today to see the development of semitic religion in its global and historical context. Once we escape the delusion that its earliest stage provides its real essence, we will be able to see that it is a continually developing set of diverse traditions. It is very helpful to trace the developments of religion, and to try to understand why it is so diverse (though we should expect it to be diverse, in the same way that human cultures are).

But the correct way to study religion is to study its most developed forms, not its primitive beginnings. And it should be studied in many different cultural settings, not as some sort of abstract and fixed set of doctrines, as though religion could be separated from its cultural contexts, and as though a religion with one name (like 'Christianity') is therefore the same thing in all the hundreds of different cultures in which it has existed. That is the gift the late nineteenth-century anthropologists gave us. Despite the fact that their specific conclusions were much too general and negative, and were based on little evidence and an excess of imagination, it is a valuable and illuminating gift. Like Aristotle in natural science, they were wrong on almost everything they said (in their case, about the origins of religion), but at least they were beginning to move in the right direction.

Part One
Religion and violence

Chapter 1
The causes of violence

On avoiding naive ideas

It is clearly impossible in one book to consider all the varieties of religion that exist. So I am just going to make a stipulative definition, and say that by 'religion' I will mean just what we might find in books about the 'world religions' – organised sets of institutions, which usually have professional spokespeople for setting out what they believe and for conducting various ritual practices involved in their beliefs. And I shall consider them in some of the variety of forms we find actually existing in the contemporary world. We need to remember that there are many other things usually called religions besides these, and I am not going to discuss them at all.

Even then, of course, the complexity of the whole thing is rather bewildering. If you set out to criticise modern Roman Catholicism, you will find many Protestants, many traditional Catholics, and many more radical Catholics, who will agree with you; and if you set out to criticise anything at all, you will find some member of the Church of England (my own church, so I am free to criticise it!) who will agree with you. So I am going to have to be a little more specific, and focus on some main institutions as key examples.

It is worth noting once more, before I leave this subject, how misleading the Shorter Oxford English Dictionary definition of religion is. An educated contemporary Christian or Buddhist would be very unhappy with saying that they were primarily concerned with 'a superhuman controlling power'. Buddhists generally deny that there is any such power, and Christians, who do think there is a God, would deplore the implication that God is an extra-terrestrial from Betelgeuse, who directs earthly affairs with the aid of his magic ray-gun.

I have every sympathy with the compilers of dictionaries, who have to try to get a very general definition that might fit every possible cause – quite impossible, as has just been seen, in the case of religion. I guess that in this case the compiler just gave up, had a drink, and put in something to keep the editor happy. But this seems to be another case in which the most naive idea gets taken to be the definition of a whole range of differing and often extremely sophisticated concepts. Some (not all) Buddhists think there are enlightened human beings (*Bodhisattvas*) who, after their earthly deaths, help believers to achieve lives of mindfulness and compassion. These beings are superhuman, in the sense of having more than normal levels of human wisdom and compassion. But they do not control human lives, and reverence for them is in fact reverence for the values they are thought to embody.

Many contemporary Christians totally reject the idea of God as a superhuman controller. For theologian Paul Tillich, for example, God is not a particular being, but the power of Being itself, and the supreme moral ideal to be reverenced for its value, not its controlling power. Atheists may doubt whether such a notion makes sense. But at least they ought to be clear that it is not the idea of a superhuman and invisible person who makes the sun shine to order. They ought also to take some account of the fact that many major classical philosophers have been able to make sense of this idea – which may suggest that it is not simply stupid or thoughtless, at least.

It should be a basic principle of intelligent analysis that a serious attempt is made to understand the most intellectually sophisticated concepts of religious belief. Some philosophers, like Anthony Kenny, sometime President of the British

Academy, do this and still disagree with many religious ideas. But they treat religious beliefs in their best intellectual forms with care and respect and careful analysis, and with due consideration for the many different interpretations that exist. That is what a truly scientific and rational approach to religion requires.

An example of religion – the Quakers

At last, having discussed and then side-stepped the almost insuperable difficulties in saying what a religion is, I can get around to the question of whether religion is dangerous.

I hope it is clear already that saying that religion is dangerous is vacuous, unless you have in mind some specific religious institution and you are accusing that of being dangerous, either because its beliefs or its practices are dangerous, or because the very existence of the institution itself is dangerous to society.

Let me illustrate this by taking some specific examples. First consider the Society of Friends, the Quakers. The Quakers are not usually seen as dangerous. They like sitting around in circles, often saying very little. They are apt to be found demonstrating against military violence and world poverty. Their beliefs are hard to pin down, but one of them involves thinking there is an 'inner light' that convicts them of various social injustices and impels them to act to remedy such injustices on occasion.

I find it hard to think of any organisation less dangerous to society than the Quakers. But you can see how they could be regarded as dangerous by someone who thought pacifism was morally wrong – that it might be a danger to the defence of the realm. There has, I believe, been one British Minister of Defence who was a Quaker. He did not last very long in the job.

In 1984 a group of Christians from the Mennonite, Quaker and Brethren Churches in Toronto and Chicago founded the

Christian Peacemaker Teams. Their members travel to areas of war and terrorism to try to promote non-violence and reconciliation. In Baghdad at least two members, Tom Cox and Ken Bigley, have been killed, while a third, the hostage Norman Kember, was freed by the army to widespread publicity. There can be no doubt that the actions of these people, religiously motivated as they are, are heroic and self-sacrificing. It would be totally absurd to accuse them of wickedness, selfishness or moral cowardice.

Some, nevertheless, regard them as irrational and a nuisance. Dr Alan Billings of Lancaster University said that their visit to Iraq had been 'self-indulgent' and that it might have increased the danger of further kidnappings and brought the troops who tried to rescue them into needless danger. 'These peaceniks are putting everyone in danger,' said one anonymous commentator.

What this really shows is that there is genuine and conscientious disagreement on some important moral issues. All agree that possible goods and harms need to be seriously weighed. But when that has been done, people can still differ over the right thing to do. Some think it is worth taking great risks for the sake of witnessing against war. Others think that we must resort to violence in a just cause, and that pacifism undermines the defence of justice.

There is very little in morality that would be agreed upon by everybody. Mother Teresa is to many people a saint who cared for the dying in the slums of Calcutta when no one else would. But others regard her work, and that of her order of nuns, as possibly having a bad social effect on the Indian political system, and as a waste of resources that could be better spent elsewhere — particularly in view of her highly publicised opposition to artificial contraception.

I do not think there is any way in which Mother Teresa or the Christian Peacemaker Teams could be regarded as evil. They are pretty obviously morally heroic, going to lengths of self-sacrifice most of us come nowhere near. But they could still be regarded as morally mistaken or useless.

However, it would be a perverted mind that regarded such heroism as dangerous. If you agree with the stand taken by these moral heroes, you will think that this religious group is one of the best things humanity can produce. Even if you disagree with their stand, you will have to admire their courage and integrity. You will have to respect that religious group for moral commitment. They might be wrong, but they are morally admirable.

At least some religious groups, then, produce moral goodness of a very high order. Their members are deserving of our admiration, even if we disagree with their beliefs. Disagreement on moral beliefs is something we just have to live with as human beings, whether we are religious or not. And there is one thing to be said for the Quakers. However strongly we disagree with them, at least we know they are not going to kill us.

A second case – Al Qaida

But how far can moral disagreement go? Let me take another case; that of the Muslim terrorist group, Al Qaida. It would be widely regarded in the West as very dangerous. It is dedicated to using indiscriminate violence to cause extreme terror in order to gain its ends. Yet obviously its members and sympathisers do not regard it as evil. They regard it as a force for justice in a radically unjust world, and a force for truth in the face of the atheism and nihilism of the West.

Good and harm do not stand as self-evident and agreed truths, so that we can all neutrally assess whether various acts do good or harm. Quakers and militant Islamists have different ideas of good and harm. Of course militant Islamists would agree that they kill people. But they would say that is good, because it will help to destroy the evil empire of the West. Before we rush to say that is absurd, remember that American bombs, which kill indiscriminately and in huge numbers causing almost indescribable pain and suffering, are not thought by most Americans to be evil. They do terrible things, but their use, it is claimed, was necessary to bring down the tyranny of Saddam Hussein.

Now there is a difference between doing something terrible as part of a struggle for the sake of a greater good (something every soldier who kills in battle has to do), and doing something that you know to be evil. An example of pure evil would be torturing a child just because you enjoy it. You have no greater good in mind. You just get pleasure out of seeing children scream. That is evil, and it exists.

If religion were evil, it would aim at no good. Its devotees would act simply for the sake of pleasure or self-interest, or simply to destroy what makes for the happiness or well-being of others. That is malevolence. There may be malevolent religions – devil-worship or 'black magic', the worship of destructive power for its own sake, is perhaps one of them. Malevolence, however, is not usually associated with religious belief. Serial killers and rapists do not normally claim to be inspired by religion. Malevolence is more usually associated with a belief in the survival of the strong through total war, or just with hatred of life and the world in general.

It is when people feel that life is pointless, that there is no point in trying to be good, that existence itself is some sort of cruel joke or regrettable accident, that they surrender to sadistic and destructive impulses. In short, it is lack of faith in the value of existence and in the possibility of goodness that is likely to lead to pure evil. And if there is one thing that the world religions are united on, it is the insistence (in the Abrahamic faiths) that existence is good, or (in Buddhist traditions) that even if existence involves suffering, release is possible by practising compassion and renouncing possessive desire. Religion cannot be the source of all evil. For it systematically opposes the hatred of existence – and that is the source of pure evil, if anything is.

We have to say, however reluctantly, that Al Qaida is not

purely evil in that sense. It aims at good, at obedience to God and passion for God's truth, and it hates only God's enemies. A parallel case might be the National Socialism of the German Third Reich. It aimed at the welfare of the German people, at what they thought would be a just and healthy society, and at the unity of Europe. Many ordinary Germans were devoted to the cause. They had suffered the humiliation of the Treaty of Versailles. They had endured near-starvation and the loss of pride and power. Now Hitler offered them pride again, and self-confidence and an ordered society.

The tragedy of Germany was that the Jews, the handicapped, homosexuals, gypsies and the mentally ill were being systematically exterminated. Large groups of humans were regarded as sub-human, and the whole economy was based on military might and the forced subjugation of other nations. How could anyone think that was good?

At the Nuremberg trials of war criminals, the prosecution argued that no one could sincerely have thought it was good. They must either have ignored what was happening, to an extent that was culpable, or they must really have known that unrestricted exercise of the will to power and the elimination of the unfit were wrong.

So we might argue that members of Al Qaida must really know that God does not hate non-Muslims, that it is wrong to kill the innocent, and that hatred is always forbidden by a God of mercy and compassion. I would argue that, and so would the vast majority of Muslims. But the power of self-deception is strong. It is very easy for people to convince themselves that evil is good.

Self-deceit in morality and religion

I recently saw a white Afrikaaner, J. P. Botha, say on television that since all eight people in Noah's ark were white, and all humans were descended from them, the blacks must be 'animals of the Veldt', and not human at all. This is such an extraordinary statement that it is almost impossible for a non-racist to understand how anyone could believe it. Yet the man's wife burst into tears at the thought that the television interviewer could not share this belief, and so was presumably, she thought, excluded from eternal life.

What can you say about cases like that? The evidence is easily available for establishing the full humanity of blacks, browns, yellows and whites. Even if it were not, it is pretty clear that the mental capacities of blacks are such that they possess whatever intelligence and moral capacity are needed to be 'made in the image of God'. Moreover, common human sympathy and compassion, not to mention rationality, would rule out reducing blacks to servant or slave status just because of their colour. And the Bible, for what that is worth, actually says nothing about the colour of Noah, whose family might well all have been black before some of them later turned white (with cold, perhaps, when they got to the Netherlands). 'I am black and beautiful,' says the Song of Solomon (Song of Songs 1:5), but J. P. Botha obviously has not noticed.

It all seems so obvious to most of us that we wonder how reasonable people could be blind to it. But before we condemn this viewpoint completely, we might do well to remember two things. First, that any national politician who did not promise to put the national interest first, before the interest of any other nation, would probably never get elected. We all seem to approve of national selfishness, though there is no reason why our nation or race should be privileged above others. And second, that even though we know many animals are conscious and feel pain, many humans would not hesitate to hunt or torture them just for fun. To cause pain to any sentient creature just for fun seems morally abominable. Yet often we simply do not think morally. We put the interest of humans, or of our own race, or of our own family, or sometimes even of ourselves, first –

and we justify that by inventing 'moral' reasons for doing so.

For example, we justify putting our own families first because, we say, that shows the importance of 'family values', of loyalty and honour. We make these into virtues and say that we are being selflessly devoted to duty, for we put honour and loyalty before self-interest.

This, of course, is a half-truth, and what is wrong is making it into the whole truth. We do have a duty to care for our families. But that duty does not outweigh every other, and it does not mean that we can treat all other families as unworthy of any consideration.

Yet in Nazi Germany, loyalty to the nation and to the Führer was proclaimed as a virtue that called for total self-sacrifice, and a virtue that stood higher than all others. I think it is possible that some people, brought up and rigorously trained in such a system, might have genuinely come to believe in the principle of 'my country right or wrong'. But actually there were some giveaways that should have alerted even them to the fact that something was very wrong.

Nationalist diatribes were filled with hate, with a sense of grievance, and with a desire for revenge for past humiliations. That is not a good basis for making decisions about what is really right or wrong.

Jews were being publicly attacked and made into objects of derision. A grotesque stereotype of 'the Jew' was substituted for detailed knowledge of actual Jews. When a whole class of people is made into an object of hatred, not for their individual crimes, but because of some alleged 'general character' they are all supposed to share, that is a sign that opinion is being manipulated – and we need to ask why.

The ideology of Hitler was readily accessible, and it should have been clear to any reader of that turgid volume *Mein Kampf* that Hitler's basic beliefs were in the will to power, in eliminating the weak, in military dominance, and in the superiority of the Aryan race. It is more than a little odd to uphold loyalty and honour as basic moral values when the very foundations of morality are being undermined by a naked appeal to power.

Moreover, could anyone who was seriously concerned about morality genuinely believe that loyalty to one's own nation and its honour are the highest moral virtues, to which all others must be subordinated? There is, of course, some virtue in loyalty to family and to nation, but if morality means anything at all, such loyalty cannot be the highest virtue. Any appeal to what is morally good must be an appeal to what is good for anyone, not just to what is good for me, for my kinship group or for my nation. Thinking seriously about morality means thinking about what is good for its own sake, and about how as many people as possible can obtain such good. Any morality that does not do so is counterfeit; it is some form of self-interest or of the will to power masquerading as virtue, and perverting our moral sense.

So we have some tests for serious moral beliefs. They must not be founded on hatred or vindictiveness; they must not propagate negative stereotypes of others or inflated estimates of our own importance; they must not be founded on self-interest or on the will to power; and they must express a serious concern for the well-being of all.

National Socialism in twentieth-century Germany failed all these tests. For that reason, we may well doubt that any reflective people could have really believed National Socialism was morally good. But most people are not very reflective. They are easily influenced by peer-group pressure. They do not get too concerned with politics unless forced to do so. And they have a naive trust in the wisdom of their political leaders. We may therefore excuse them; but we can never condone their beliefs. Those beliefs are evil, even if they seem to be good.

If we now look at Al Qaida and its activities, it is perfectly clear that its ideology is founded on hatred and on a stereotypical idolisation of Muslims and demonisation of 'Kaffirs' (unbelievers). It manifests the will to power, in the drive to dominate the world. And it is indifferent to the well-being of most of the world's population, who are to be eliminated or converted. The beliefs of Al Qaida are unequivocally evil.

But are they not religious beliefs? Yes, they are. There are some unequivocally evil religious beliefs. In the discussion of National Socialism, it is obvious that there are also some unequivocally evil non-religious beliefs. What makes beliefs evil is not religion, but hatred, ignorance, the will to power, and indifference to others.

In both Nazism and Al Qaida, there are some people who seem to think their beliefs are moral and good, though they are clearly mistaken, as the Nuremberg prosecutors held. We need some explanation of how people can come to have such perverse 'moral' beliefs. In the case of Al Qaida we do not have to search very far for such an explanation. In a report by the Joint Intelligence Committee made to the British Home Secretary in April 2006, the main causes said to be conducive to membership of terrorist organisations are cited as: opposition to the war in Iraq, economic deprivation, social exclusion, and disaffection with community leaders. None of these are religious causes. They become associated with Islam through a series of rather implausible connections. The attack on Saddam Hussein and his (non-religious) rule is equated with an attack on Islam; this is seen as signifying approval of Israeli attacks on Palestinians and hostility against Muslims in general; discrimination against immigrants is equated with discrimination against Muslims; and (despite the hostility of Shi'a and Sunni Muslims to one another) Islam is seen as engaged in a battle with a colonialist, economically dominant, morally and religiously bankrupt 'West'.

None of these claims can stand up to close scrutiny. But they all tie together to form a 'grand conspiracy theory' of history, and provide an identifiable enemy against whom the rage, envy, bitterness and vindictiveness of people who feel unjustly attacked and oppressed can be directed.

There are many such conspiracy theories in the world, but

they are nearly all concerned with social and economic inequalities rather than with religious issues. What is needed to explain the resort to terrorist activity is close investigation of such social and economic matters. Of course we want to know what it is in religion that allows it to be used as a 'moral' cloak for evil actions. But the sad truth is that almost any human beliefs and institutions can be utilised for evil ends, given the existence of deeply rooted hatreds and genuine injustices.

Texts of violence

Islam can be used to stir up hatred and the desire for revenge – as can Christianity and Judaism in the right economic circumstances – because the religion was founded in opposition to preceding mores and beliefs, and because from time to time it had to fight to preserve its integrity or its very existence. So there are texts and traditions that justify the use of violence in self-defence, and that castigate enemies of the faith. In Judaism you could always pull out ancient and obsolete regulations from the book of Deuteronomy that seem to recommend genocide of the Canaanites, or that seem to give the Jews ownership of the land between the Nile and the Euphrates.

In Christianity texts have been found to justify regarding 'the Jews' as Christ-killers, or even for compelling people to become Christians by force.

Such texts exist, but the real question to ask is what makes people pull them out and make them decisive texts to be literally applied in the very different circumstances of the modern world. It is not anything in the religion itself that makes them do so. For each tradition has developed sophisticated ways of overriding those texts with other and usually later interpretations that stress what is quite clearly more basic – the command of God to have compassion and mercy.

Any Muslim today who cites the Qur'an or Hadith (recorded sayings of the Prophet) in support of the view that Islam should forcibly convert the world to Islam stands in opposition to every scholarly tradition in Islam. In such traditions, *jihad*, meaning striving, is primarily interpreted as the striving of the heart to obey God. Only secondarily is *jihad* taken to refer to the use of violence. And then it is, by general Muslim scholarly consent, confined to the defence of Islam or Islamic countries against unjust attack – a doctrine that most moralists, both religious and secular, accept.

Any Jew who called for the conquest of Egypt, Syria and Iraq by Israel would be regarded as demented by virtually all rabbis. Israel is, for a start, a secular state that does not appeal to religion for its right to exist. From an orthodox religious standpoint, the 'promise' of the land from Dan to Beersheba has been rendered obsolete, along with the destruction of the Temple and the priesthood. It provides no justification for aggression against Palestine. Indeed, the biblical injunctions to care for the 'foreigner' who lives in the Holy Land outweigh any ordinances about an ancient war of conquest that took place (if it actually happened at all) thousands of years ago.

Similarly, the vast majority of Christian churches regret the Crusades and the persecution of the Jews as complete misunderstandings of Jesus' command to love your enemies and to seek reconciliation and peace, not to pursue a way of revenge and anger.

Religious scriptures can be misused. But such misuses can be identified by the fact that they ignore the weightier matters of scriptures – the love of God and neighbour, and the search for compassion and mercy – and choose texts taken out of context and applied without any sense of history or concern for general traditions of interpretation.

In short, there are texts that can be found and used by those who are filled with rage and hatred. But they can be so used only by ignoring the scholarly traditions of interpretation in the religion, by a refusal to engage in reflective discussion of the whole scripture, and by basing a careful selection of texts on considerations of hatred and intolerance.

If it is argued that religious texts breed intolerance, the question that must be asked is: what causes people to choose those texts, which according to the general scholarly consensus of religious scholars were for situations long in the past, and which have since been overridden both by other specific texts and by the general sense of scripture? The answer to that question can only be given by detailed examination of the social contexts in which such choices are made, usually contexts of social and economic injustice and deprivation. In short, it is hatred and intolerance that cause religious texts to be chosen to give a sham moral support to perverted natural inclinations. It is not religion that causes intolerance. It is intolerance that uses religion to give alleged 'moral' support to the real cause of intolerance – hatred of those perceived or imagined to be oppressors or threats to one's own welfare.

Religion and evil

The leaders of such movements can fairly be accused of using moral and religious language as a cloak for evil and irreligious ends, and for them there is no moral or religious defence. There are also many people who simply let evil happen – partly because it achieves some things they want, and partly because they are not directly threatened by the evil that occurs. For them too there is little defence. The only people who could be exempted from a charge of knowing complicity in evil are those who have been so brainwashed or blinded by ignorance or emotion that they really do come to believe that evil is good. That may be true both in non-religious systems like Nazism or Marxist-Leninism, and in religious systems like Al Qaida or the Japanese cult of Aum Supreme Truth, responsible for the sarin gas attack in Tokyo in 1995, which killed twelve people and left thousands in need of treatment.

But there is this big difference between the case of the Nazis and that of Al Qaida. In the end, the leading Nazis knew what they were doing. They knew they were replacing morality with power, that morality was the invention of the weak, and that strength and victory were all that mattered. But militant Islamists do not know what they are doing. Of course they think they do. They think they are replacing human morality with God's sheer amoral power, and that God wills strength and victory to Islam at any cost. But in fact the God of Islam is defined by the Qur'an, and the Qur'an defines that God as a God of compassion and mercy, of justice and righteousness. The God of Islam is not a God of raw and amoral power. He is, like the God of Abraham (whom he is said to be), a God who may be severe in judgment, calling all to account for their deeds, but he is also a God of compassion, concerned for the well-being of all creation. Indeed, there are reliable traditions that say that all people will eventually find Paradise. So Muslim militants are wrong about the God they claim to worship, and they are demonstrably wrong, according to their own most holy text.

Al Qaida is a religious organisation founded on hatred, ignorance, the will to power, and indifference to God's creation. It is condemned by the words of its own alleged religion. So the difference between the Nazis and Al Qaida is this: the Nazis had no internal way of correcting their own evil ideology. But militant Islam has an internal way of correcting its evil ideology; and that way is by reference to Islam itself. Nazism was a clear-sighted rejection of morality. Militant Islam is a corruption of Islam, which is the worship of and obedience to a supreme reality of perfect goodness. Militant Islam is dangerously wrong about its idea of perfect goodness. But Islam contains the materials to correct that corruption.

My conclusion is that all human beings, religious or not, are prone to evil. Human beings are dangerous, and anything they believe or do will probably go terribly wrong at some point. The question is: how can we best guard against that? One of the best safeguards is a set of beliefs that convicts humans of wrongdoing and promises them a reconciliation with a personal being of supreme goodness. That will not eliminate corruption, but it will be a resource that exposes corruption for what it is, and constantly recalls humans to seek goodness.

Religion does not lead to corruption. Human nature leads to corruption. If we let human beings into our religion, it is going to get corrupted. The major world religions all contain resources to expose corruption and to call humans to repentance. We would therefore expect them to go wrong from time to time – and militant Islam is going spectacularly wrong at present. But we would also expect them to have the resources for redirection towards goodness.

My Muslim friends completely agree with me about this. Speaking for my own faith, Christians certainly believe in a God who condemns all hatred and anger, who commands us to love our neighbours as ourselves, and even to love our enemies, who forgives our moral shortcomings, and who promises that goodness will not finally be defeated by evil, either in religion or out of it. This is as far removed as possible from the Marxist-Leninist or Fascist rejection of objective morality, and the pitiless embrace of the sheer will to power. If there is a root of evil that became a terrifying force that almost brought the world to destruction in the first half of the twentieth century, it is the anti-religious ideologies of Germany and Russia, North Vietnam and North Korea. It takes almost wilful blindness to invert this historical fact, and to suppose that the religions that were persecuted and crushed by these brutal forces are the real sources of evil in the world.

Religion – the cause of evil?

I have argued that there is such a thing as pure malevolence – hatred of life, of others and of oneself. This powerful destructive force is very far from being condoned by any major religion. Most religions explicitly condemn and oppose hatred of life.

There is also a sort of pseudo-goodness, in which hatred, the desire for power, and indifference to others are disguised as moral goods — for instance, of loyalty, patriotism and honour. Some religious movements are of this sort, though the main religious traditions contain internal criticisms of their positions. But many movements like this are not religious, but ethnic, nationalist or imperialist.

Thirdly, among social institutions that aim at good, there are genuine differences of opinion about what is truly good — about, for instance, whether violence can be justified or whether it is always wrong. These differences do not usually divide on religious lines, but tend to exist among both the religious and the unreligious. Religions do not create the differences, and once they exist, religious believers are to be found on both sides.

So far, then, it seems that religions can be morally corrupt, but so can secular movements like Communism or Fascism. And religions can have controversial moral beliefs, but those beliefs are likely to be controversial and disputed among non-religious people also. It looks as if religions are not the causes of evil, but they do naturally share in the general moral state of the societies in which they exist.

Chapter 2
The corruptibility of all things human

The ever-present possibility of corruption

It is very difficult to think of any organised human activity that could not be corrupted, or that is free from deep disputes about the right way to go about doing things.

Think of liberal democracy, for example. A popular definition of democracy is 'government by the people for the people'. In a democracy, ordinary citizens have some control over the laws of their state. A minimal definition of liberalism is that people should be free to express their opinions and beliefs. As the nineteenth-century English philosopher John Stuart Mill put it, a liberal society is one in which freedom of expression, interests and assembly is protected.

So a liberal democracy is a form of government in which people are free to express political beliefs, to form political parties to represent their interests, and to exercise some control over the running of their society.

To many people it seems obvious that liberal democracy is a wholly good thing and a form of government that should be accepted by everyone in the world. They would be aghast to be told that liberal democracy was the 'root of all evil'. Indeed I myself think that would be an absurdly extreme position to take. Yet liberal democracy can go wrong. Plato said that democracy was the second worst form of government, 'the rule of the mob'. Adolf Hitler was democratically elected. What if you lived in a deeply racist society in Africa, where a vast majority wished to eliminate white people? You could allow everyone to express their views, knowing that the majority would always win. By a popular vote, the white minority could quickly be eliminated – even though they were free to protest about it.

Liberalism can be interpreted as freedom to do whatever you like – including exterminating people you do not like. And democracy could leave minorities without any real power, even though theoretically they are free to play a part in government.

A little thought will show that liberal democracy is a very delicate thing. It can very easily get out of hand and lead to genocide or tyranny – as long as the majority want to be led by a 'Great Leader', and can be deluded into thinking that is for their own greater good.

What you have to say is that liberal democracy is a good thing as long as it does not lead to these terrible outcomes – but that is blindingly obvious. Most liberal democrats are aware of this, and propose democracy not as a perfect political system but simply as the least bad way of preventing things from going terribly wrong. But even democracy is dangerous, and it is precisely when we do not realise the dangers that things can begin to go wrong.

You may say this is just theorising. In practice liberal democracies do good and prevent the evil of tyrannical or oppressive governments. But at least for some years in Germany and in South Africa they did not. Both produced deeply racist societies. Even in democratic countries like the United States, there are real questions to be asked about the role permanent minorities are able to play in democratic elections that require huge amounts of money to support candidates, and that use every means of propaganda to slant statistics, manipulate information and influence opinion. Although we hope it will never happen, it is possible that a racist government might in future be elected that reverses all the gains that have been made in recent years, and begins to persecute racial minorities. Or it could become a widespread belief that everyone should be free to follow their own strongest desires. But since freedom, in this context, might only mean that the state should not stop you from doing what you want, organised crime and big business – probably in cooperation with one another – could exercise their freedom to run society in a way that kept thousands of citizens in poverty and want, or even sent potentially troublesome cases off to fight wars in faraway countries.

The lesson is that anti-religious corruptions and religious corruptions are both possible. There is no magic system or belief, not even belief in liberal democracy, which can be guaranteed to prevent it.

The battle against corruption in religion and politics

Some people believe that liberal democracy in America has already been corrupted. I would regard that view as perverse. But I do suspect that America, like Britain, is only prevented from sinking into social chaos and corruption by the preservation of a strong moral sense that individuals matter, and that some concern for the flourishing of all people should be a mark of acceptable social policy.

Philip Roth's novel, *The Plot Against America*, outlines the way America early in the Second World War could have become pro-German and anti-Jewish if Roosevelt had not been elected for a third term. In the novel, American good sense and concern for human rights prevail. But it provides a convincing case for the possibility that a whole freedom-loving society could find itself on the track to racism and a Fascist-style leadership.

So liberal democracy is dangerous. That it produces a more or less just society is more a matter of good fortune than of good judgment. Something more than a commitment to liberal democracy is needed to produce a just and morally oriented society. An important part of that 'something more' is a public commitment to respect for human values, for fairness and for the importance of some form of fulfilment for each person, as far as that is possible. Where such respect is lacking, liberal democracy will fail to preserve a realistic freedom for everyone, and will fail to ensure that the rights of minorities are respected.

It turns out that liberal democracy is in very much the same boat as religion. Some democracies will be corrupted if the will of the majority is for the suppression of minorities and foreigners. Many democracies will be crippled by deep disputes about who should govern, and what their policies should be. And democracy itself turns out to be insufficient to guarantee a morally just society, if there is not a consensus about the importance and nature of justice.

It should be perfectly obvious, however, that we can admit that liberal democracy can be dangerous, and that in some cases it has become corrupt, without conceding that liberal democracy is a bad thing, or that we would be better off without it. The same is true of religion. The reasonable thing to say is that liberal democracy is a good thing, as long as it is complemented by a strong moral impulse to consider the welfare of all people. In human life that can never be absolutely guaranteed. But it would be wise for any society to seek the most effective means possible for encouraging and motivating a moral sensibility in its members. This means some form of systematic moral education – of inculcating a sense of the value of personhood, the pursuit of individual virtue and the common good.

There can be little doubt that one major source of such moral education is religion. The effectiveness of such a system of education cannot be guaranteed. And in any given society there will exist blind spots and limitations of moral vision. Deep differences of viewpoint can never be eliminated, and from the vantage point of the present it takes no genius to discern the limitations of the past. In Europe slavery was accepted until the Brussels Act of 1890, which prohibited the African slave trade. Women could take no part in democratic elections in Britain until 1918, when women over thirty were allowed to vote. Capital punishment was widely applauded, and was only abolished in Britain in 1969. There has been, we would say (well, naturally we would), moral progress. There has certainly been significant moral change, and it can be traced in legal enactments and decisions over recorded history.

It would be absurd to condemn the British legal system because it used to condone the death penalty for stealing sheep. That was then. This is now. Somehow the system has produced improvements, and will, we hope, continue to do so.

How can we rationally deny the same judgment to a system of religion? We cannot judge its present morality on ancient and superseded enactments of the past, sometimes of the very far past. We should rather acknowledge that it has changed, and hope that it will go on doing so, in a continually more humane direction.

In the campaigns against slavery, Christians such as Wilberforce played a leading role. In protests against capital punishment, many Christians were vociferous campaigners. And women's suffrage leaders included many Christian believers, such as Josephine Butler, one of the first signatories of the petition to parliament for women's suffrage and a heroic campaigner for women's rights in the late nineteenth century. So a good claim can be made, not that these moral advances were solely sponsored by Christians, and not that all Christians supported them, but that they were supported by many Christian believers, that some Christians played a leading – indeed defining – part in campaigns for them, and that religious grounds were brought forward in their support.

Connections between religion, politics and morality

Naturally, in religion as in politics, there are conservatives who defend the status quo as well as radicals who seek change. It is impossible to answer the question: does religious belief tend to make people more conservative or more radical? It depends on the religious belief and on the political and moral views of the people in question. What is needed is in-depth social analysis, and more of that needs to be done.

Some sorts of religion in some sorts of social context will attract people of conservative temperament. It is not totally surprising that in the eighteenth century the Church of England, many of whose clergy were the sons of the gentry, attracted conservative landowners. They attained positions of influence in church appointments, and so the institution came to have a predominantly conservative character.

On the other hand, dissenting churches were meeting places for like-minded persons who were much more radical in outlook, long before they got into a religious group. Once they were in, naturally their children would be influenced by this general tone, and were much more likely to be in favour of reform and support for socially excluded groups. None of them were permitted to attend Oxford or Cambridge Universities, for example, so they naturally attracted members who were largely outside the established centres of social power.

In the late twentieth century Church of England clergy had become notably underpaid, and were not normally connected by birth with the upper classes. The first Labour government of 1945 transformed social conditions in Britain, and a new group of educated men who were definitely not public school educated (that means educated in private schools, for some odd and typically British reason) came to prominence. The Church of England has in consequence become left of centre, and conservatives often feel rather uneasy in it. So we might say that joining the Church of England today may well make people rather more radical (in favour of Fair Trade, the cancelling of Third World debt, and conservationist environmental measures, for example). But of course they are unlikely to join unless they are quite disposed to be radical in the first place.

The dissenting churches, for their part, are now fully enfranchised, but as a result they have lost much of their social importance as a non-establishment focus of radical thought. Indeed they have been out-radicalised by many non-church-based movements like Deep Ecology and lesbian and gay pressure groups. They have come to look rather staid and middle class, and a new group of successful community churches has arisen, that takes notably conservative attitudes, especially on sex and the family. This is still a form of dissent from establishment thinking, but ironically in this very different social context dissent takes the form of supporting unfashionably conservative views, both religiously and politically. Someone who joins a community church today is likely to be presented with conservative views that may well reinforce their conservatism. But again, they are unlikely to join unless that is their predisposition anyway.

The reason why it is not possible to give a general answer to the question, 'Does religion make people more conservative or more radical?' is that religious institutions are made up of people who already have certain moral and political opinions, and will seek to mould the institution accordingly. Their children in turn will be moulded in part by those institutions, but they will also encounter many different attitudes in the general culture. So, apart from a very detailed analysis of particular histories and cases, there is little that can be usefully said in general about the social effects of religion. (Despite this, I will return to the subject in chapter 10.)

In some contexts, religious institutions can become centres of social dissent, and even revolution. During the years of Communist occupation, the Catholic Church in Poland became a focus for anti-Soviet feeling, and was a major cause of the collapse of Communism in Poland. It was a radical social force. But since that happened, the Polish Catholic Church has come to be seen by many as a conservative force trying to enforce strict sexual control and traditional family values. Radical nationalist groups have even appealed to 'Catholic loyalty' in attacks on Muslims, foreign workers and immigrants – on all things that they feel to be alien cultural influences. Thus in a very short space of time a major religious institution can move from being a focus of radical political thought to being a morally ambiguous defender of conservative national values.

The lesson is: do not generalise in abstract terms. See religious movements in their historical and social context. And acknowledge the inescapable diversity of human political, moral and religious attitudes. This might make it sound as if religious beliefs are not primarily important and we can explain religion very well simply in social terms. But that would be the opposite error. It is an error to see religion just in social terms. But it is equally an error to think that religions add nothing to the social context. They do add something, but what they add depends on the context and on who is doing the adding.

The distinctive contribution of religion

The most basic thing developed religions contribute to social attitudes is a sense of the sacred, of something so good that it is worthy of unconditional reverence. This sense of the sacred calls people to express something of that goodness in their own lives, and to commit their lives to gaining greater knowledge of that good.

The God of Judaism, Christianity and Islam is a being of justice, mercy and loving-kindness, who commands humans to be just, merciful and kind, and who promises those who are just a life beyond death in union with absolute goodness. The Supreme Self of many Indian religions is a reality of supreme wisdom and bliss, knowledge of which leads people to see that all things are part of the Supreme Self and worthy of reverence, and union with which can be attained by lives of compassion and non-attachment. The Tao or Way of Heaven in some East Asian religions is a basic moral order written into the structure of the universe, calling people to live in accordance with that order of justice, and laying down ways of life that will bring fulfilment, mindfulness and inner happiness.

There are other religions than these. But every major religion stresses the objective existence of moral ideals, the importance of moral conduct, and the possibility for human individuals and societies of attaining a good and happy life. Religions are among the chief agents of moral education in most countries. But what religions say in spelling out these basic beliefs will depend on the historical and social context in which they say it.

It is quite wrong to think that religions have some sort of complete and self-enclosed system of morality, which they insist on applying whatever the society in which they exist is like. That is perhaps one of the disadvantages of using the word 'religion', that it may lead people to think that there is one unchanging set of moral rules that a 'religion' has, and that those rules will pay no attention to the culture and society in which the religion exists.

A reasonable knowledge of history is sufficient to dispel any such notion. In the case of Christianity, one of the most obvious examples is usury (lending money at interest). This was formally condemned by the Third Lateran Council in 1179. It was not until the nineteenth century that the Catholic Church officially allowed the practice, upon which the whole of modern banking in the West is based. No Christian today would dream of condemning lending at interest as immoral, and many American churches exist on interest from their endowments. This is a clear example of a moral rule changing because of changes in social and economic conditions in society.

Another, equally striking, is the notion of the freedom to express and practise religious beliefs. Pope Pius IX condemned this in his *Syllabus of Errors* of 1864, which condemned no fewer than eighty errors of modern thought, including liberalism and the freedom to practise any non-Catholic religion (in a Catholic country, presumably). But the Second Vatican Council, in the 1960s, asserted such freedom as a fundamental right and a clear implication of the gospel[1]. Between those two statements there had been a general social change in Europe that had thrown doubt on the claims of any political or religious authority to impose its beliefs on all members of society, and had come to believe that the freedom to criticise was an aid to finding truth, not a symptom of moral depravity.

What would be radically misleading would be to oppose 'religion' to 'culture', as though they were different and competing forces. In any given culture, there are conservatives who wish to preserve traditions and practices that protect treasured values, and there are radicals who wish to change old traditions for the sake of having a more just or fair society. In democracies, this often becomes formalised in the existence of conservative and reforming 'Parties', whose members generally ally themselves with one of these attitudes. It is just the same in religious institutions. Conservatives basically wish to keep things the way they are, and reformers wish to challenge tradition, usually in the name of justice or of new moral perceptions.

Are religious groups, as such, more conservative than secular groups? That too depends on circumstances. In France, before the Revolution, the Catholic Church generally allied itself with the *ancien régime*, with the ruling aristocracy and social hierarchy. But there were hundreds of Catholic priests who did not do so, and who were initially sympathetic to the Revolution – until it began killing priests.

The Catholic Church in France was itself an ancient institution, governed by elderly men, usually of aristocratic lineage, and heavily involved with the ruling elite of the country. It was these social facts about the religious institution that decreed that the church and political conservatism would largely be in alliance with one another – and that the poor parish clergy would as a rule not share those views. There was little in the documents of the New Testament or in the teaching of Jesus to support an alliance between wealth, privilege and a Christian gospel which contains as crucial sentiments: 'Blessed are the poor' and 'He has cast down the mighty from their seats, and the rich he has sent empty away'. We have to explain the conservatism of the Catholic Church in eighteenth-century France by drawing attention to the class affiliations of the leaders of that church, which operated to countermand some of the religion's basic teachings.

There is a stark contrast between the situation in France and that in Britain during the same period. In France socialism was largely seen as an anti-Catholic force, ranged against the *ancien régime* and the defence of social and religious hierarchy. But in England the birth of socialism was very often associated with or even inspired by Christian idealism. This was partly due to the fact that the Church of England, after an unsuccessful struggle to retain a monopoly of religious power, permitted religious dissent. The dissenting Protestant churches usually identified with social forces that did not belong to the establishment, and so there grew up a religious base for social policies that were reforming and often radical. The non-conformist tradition in England has been of tremendous social significance. But to explain that fact it is not enough to point to something inherent in the religion itself, in the abstract. We have to look at the social and historical context, and note how the Church of England, being by nature a dissenting church itself (dissenting from the Church of Rome), had no really convincing argument for opposing the existence of other dissenting churches. Then by observation of the social and economic position of the leaders of the dissenting churches, a connection between reforming politics and religious belief becomes intelligible, and almost predictable (insofar as anything in social science is truly predictable).

Religion and social values

A religious creed or core set of beliefs might be seen as rather like the American Constitution. It is a foundation document that can be interpreted in different ways in different contexts. It lays down limits of reasonable interpretation, but does not dictate the exact interpretation that will be taken at a specific time – judges, scholars or religious leaders do that, and they can differ quite sharply in their interpretations.

This is true of all human social institutions, not just of religious institutions. It is never helpful to ask what 'a religion', in the abstract, teaches. What you have to investigate is how, given the history and the structure of a given society, a specific set of religious beliefs is going to be interpreted by the sort of individuals who are responsible for the interpretation.

If religion is dangerous in a specific society, it is because of some social, historical or political problem that exists, and with which some strands of a specific religion can be correlated, however implausibly. In British society in 2006, immigrant communities often feel excluded, relatively deprived and despised. Since large groups of them come from Muslim countries such as Pakistan and Bangladesh, they can find strands of Islam that help them to feel pride in their identity, and to meet contempt with defensive isolation and resentment.

In a similar way, the British National Party, devoted basically to keeping Britain white, often tries to make an alliance with Christianity – as the Ku Klux Klan did in the United States. This alliance is almost totally incomprehensible to outsiders, but it is done by claiming that 'white' civilisation is based on Christian values, which must be defended against attack. It is true that most English people in the past have been both white and at least nominally Christian. But it is a completely invalid inference that the defence of Christian values is a defence of the Aryan race. A little more knowledge of history would quickly reveal that Christianity is a Middle Eastern faith, and the majority of Christians worldwide are not white. But Nationalists are not interested either in logic or in the facts of history. That is a good reason for saying that Nationalist racism is based on ignorance and prejudice, not on observation and reasoning. By ignoring the facts, by inventing a rose-coloured English past of jolly maypole-dancing and peaceful family values, and picturing immigrants as very different and as subversive and ignorant, a politics of hatred and fear is given a veneer of moral respectability.

Machiavelli saw this very clearly: if you wish to be evil and to get away with it, you must take great care that you appear to be committed to morality and religion, to core values of great, even cosmic importance. The distortion of evil to make it appear good is one of the first tricks of the successfully evil. So religion is one of the main weapons in the armoury of evil. It is for this reason that I would feel almost embarrassed to fly the Union flag outside my house or church, just in case some people thought I was a member of the National Front, or the British National Party.

I may indeed be patriotic, prepared to defend my country against unjust attack. But the use of the Union flag by racist groups has made it seem dubious. I similarly feel very alarmed when Nationalist groups contact me, as they have done, to enlist my support for their racist and unjust policies. It makes me wonder what I have ever said or done to make them think I would agree with them. Then I realise that it is because I have said some conservative-sounding things about religious doctrines that they think I will be a rabid Nationalist. What needs to be done is to distinguish defensible patriotism clearly from fanatical jingoism. In religion, we need to distinguish rationally defensible belief from irrational fanaticism. The intellectual laziness of those who attack religion as such is that they fail to do that. So they fall into the trap the fanatics have prepared for them. By confusing what is fanatical with what is reasonable and good, they are misled into attacking things that are good. So they become complicit in undermining attitudes and practices which really are of great social and moral value — and that is exactly what fanatics want.

Religious and social elements are tied together in a complex way. Marx was exaggerating when he said that religious (and, he thought, moral and scientific) beliefs are like the 'scum' on the surface of social processes of production and exchange. Ideas and beliefs do have an effect on the sort of socioeconomic structures that exist in specific societies. But it is an important insight that beliefs do not exist outside any socioeconomic context, and the particular form those beliefs take will correlate with the history and structure of the society in which they are embodied.

In other words, rather than asking 'Is religion dangerous?', we really need to ask, 'Is this particular religion, at this stage of its development, dangerous in this social context?' It is then obvious that the answer to the question will not always be the same. Nevertheless, I suggest that it is fairly clear to any unbiased observer that in most societies, most of the time, religion is one of the forces making both for social stability and for morally serious debate and reform. It certainly sets out to be. In subsequent chapters I will investigate how far it really is.

Chapter 3
Religion and war

Sayyid Qutb and militant Islam: a problem case

When considering the question of religion and violence, it is undoubtedly true that at the present time Islam presents a particular problem for Western secular democracies, and this case requires special consideration. The problem is that there exist Muslim groups that are committed to annihilating Western secular democracies by force or terror, and replacing them with a worldwide Islamic society under the rule of *Shari'a* or Islamic law.

One influential source for this view is Sayyid Qutb of the Muslim Brotherhood. In his 1965 book, *Milestones on the Road*[1], he writes, 'One should accept the *Shari'a* without any question and reject all other laws in any shape or form. This is Islam.' Every society is either Muslim or *jahiliyyah*. Muslim societies are those that live in complete obedience to *Shari'a*. But it turns out that 'all the societies existing in the world today are *jahili*... all these societies are unIslamic and illegal'. He defines a *jahili* society as one in which there is 'one man's lordship over another', in which the laws are man-made. That obviously includes all democracies and all political systems that legislate laws – including, apparently, all existing so-called Muslim societies. By contrast, in a truly Muslim society only God legislates laws.

There can be no compromise or even coexistence with such societies. Indeed, Qutb writes, 'There is no Islam in a land where Islam is not dominant and where its *Shari'a* is not established.' That might sound bad enough. But it gets worse: *jihad*, striving in the way of God, must take the initiative in abolishing *jahiliyyah*. It is not just a defensive war; it is the use of force to establish properly Muslim societies everywhere in the world, so that ultimately there will remain in the world only Muslims, enemies of Islam to be fought, and *Dhimmies*, those who pay tribute-money to their dominant Islamic society.

What about tolerance and lack of compulsion in religion? That will remain, writes Qutb, once people have been delivered from servitude to *jahiliyyah* into the freedom of *Shari'a*. For then no one will be forced to have Muslim beliefs – though they will rightly be forced to live under *Shari'a* law. It is Islam's duty, he writes, to exercise its 'God-given right to step forward and take control of the political authority so that it may establish the Divine system on earth'.

This undoubtedly is a religious view, and it is pretty dangerous to almost everyone, including the vast majority of Muslims, since Qutb insists that there are no truly Muslim societies, and so all societies everywhere must be annihilated or subdued. It is uncannily reminiscent of Lenin's *What is to be Done?*, which in a similar way holds that there are no true socialist societies in the world, that violent revolution is needed to establish the only true form of socialism, and that the whole world must eventually become Communist. Indeed, though Qutb opposes Communism on the ground that it is atheistic, his outlook is otherwise exactly like that of Leninist Communism. It springs from and speaks to people with a sense of oppression and economic inferiority. It sees the world as divided into two clearly identifiable groups, one wholly evil and one wholly good. The world is dominated by the evil powers, which need to be annihilated by force. It supposes that 'true believers' have access to a set of rather simple political principles that will put everything right and solve all social problems. It calls people to join a select group whose historical mission and destiny it is to save the world from evil. And it promises that the controlling forces of history (the Dialectic of History for Lenin, God for Qutb) will ensure victory for the elite band of warriors in their struggle against apparently overwhelming odds.

Ironically, it seems that many Islamic Jihadists have been strongly influenced by a basically Marxist analysis of the world situation. That analysis is that the world is radically unjust, that the undeveloped nations are kept in subjugation and economic dependence by the West, and that violent revolution is the only way to overthrow Western influence. In Marx, the claim of injustice was not some sort of appeal to morality, since for Marx there exists no objective thing called morality. It is a purely descriptive statement that one part of the world is much wealthier than the rest and is successful because it uses the natural resources and cheap labour of the rest for its own well-being. Green gardens are plentifully watered in the desert state of California, while thousands die of thirst in sub-Saharan Africa. Marxism, properly interpreted, does not blame Californians for this. But Marxism predicts that the situation is economically unstable, and that the desires of the Third World for a larger share of the world's goods will eventually cause the present economic system to be overthrown.

Nevertheless, documents like the Communist Manifesto carry the ring of moral outrage and passion for justice. 'Workers of the world unite' and 'You have nothing to lose but your chains' do not seem like descriptions and predictions, though as parts of a supposedly scientific system that is what they should be. The genius of Marxism is to offer a pretence of scientific objectivity and an unmasking of bourgeois morality as a defence of capitalist interests, alongside a passionate crusade for justice. Mix this with a system that justifies the use of destructive violence, allows expression for feelings of envy and dislike, and permits us to think of revolution and terror as morally justifiable or even obligatory – indeed as part of the inevitable progress of history towards the goal of a truly free and equitable society – and you have a potent social brew.

The clue to understanding Jihadist Islam is to see that it is a form of Islamicised Marxism, a Muslim theology of liberation that has capitulated to a secular agenda. This may seem very ironic, but it is revealed as the truth by the fact that Jihadists take no notice of Muslim tradition or of Qur'anic statements about the compassion and mercy of God. They see the world as radically unjust. This is compounded by anger at Israeli treatment of Palestinians, and at the West's perceived support of Israel and attempted control of natural resources in the Middle East. They see God's call for justice in the world. They see that there is no possibility of winning an open military conflict with the West. Then, by a Marxist inversion of Islam, they conclude that the goal of history lies in a pure Islamic society and is to be attained by violence and terror.

That, for most Muslims, is a completely unacceptable step. Islam does not, historically, promise a pure Islamic society on earth. Indeed, it foresees that the various peoples of the Book will continue to coexist. And Islam does not, for the vast majority of Muslim legal scholars, justify violence except in self-defence. To call terrorism self-defence is an irrational perspective that depends on the false premise that the West is attacking Islam as such, and on the morally prohibited practice, in traditional Islam, of killing the innocent.

It is thus not religion that causes Islamic terrorism. It is a version of Islam that has been corrupted by the most successful anti-religious movement in the twentieth century, Marxist-Leninism. What motivates such naive political attitudes is not the love of God. It is hatred of almost everyone in the world as evil, belief in very simple political solutions to intractable social problems, belief that resorting to extreme violence is a reliable means to future freedom and peace, and an intense certainty that one's own beliefs are uniquely correct and morally pure, whereas everyone else's are irrational and corrupt.

Most people, including most religious believers, Muslim and non-Muslim, think it is absurd to believe that the world is controlled by some sort of conspiracy of evil – human life is more complex than that, and human motives, while rarely purely altruistic, are also rarely purely malign. Most people know that there are no simple political solutions. Even if we could agree on exactly what *Shari'a* enjoins (which Muslims cannot), it would stand in need of constant qualification to meet varied circumstances. Violence is not a viable path to peace, and most revolutions in history have eventually ended in chaos or in tyranny. And undue certainty about the correctness of one's own views, despite almost universal rejection of them, is not usually a sign of superior knowledge or wisdom.

Qutb and traditional Islam

In Qutb's case, the fact that he is opposed to all present Muslim societies and that he rejects with special vituperation the writings of traditional Muslim scholars makes it obvious that his views are not representative of Islam. It seems that a complex set of historical and social grievances has acted upon a man with naive, uninformed and radically simplistic political and religious views, to cause him to issue a highly dangerous religio-political manifesto. The group that appeals to this manifesto also happens to do a great deal of social and welfare work in Egypt and elsewhere, especially among the poor and illiterate. This gains them the sympathy of many who primarily wish to change the economic situation in their own country, but who may also be persuaded that their ills are due to some distant influence like 'Western colonialism' or 'Jewish connivance'. In ways like this what we call 'Muslim fundamentalism' is born.

It is a dangerous religious view. But what can be done about it? One of the worst recommendations would be to eliminate Islam and Muslim belief. How could this be done – by repression, censorship, or by force? The primary object of 'fundamentalist' hostility is traditional Islam, which it regards as not being Islam at all. So to eliminate Islam (even if it could be done) would actually help the fundamentalist cause.

There is no easy solution, but three main possibilities suggest themselves. First, the grievances that cause people to take such views seriously – unemployment, discrimination, exclusion from the political process, and social injustice – should be addressed. A standing grievance for many Muslims is the way that the state of Israel treats Palestinians, and it is obviously a priority to seek some resolution of this problem that allows Israel and Palestine to coexist. Israel is a secular state, and many Palestinians are not Muslims, but this conflict has led many Muslims throughout the world to oppose 'the West' as a supporter of what they perceive to be unjust actions by Israel with regard to Palestinian Muslims. We may well think that if as much money had been expended on this problem as has been expended on the war on Iraq, there would be a better chance of finding some solution.

Second, education in religion should be a primary goal. By education I mean providing a reasonably balanced view of the tradition, its history and its variety, giving a fair assessment of its place in global history, and making clear the necessity of reflective and self-critical thought in religion. There are plenty of Muslims who do this. Al-Azhar University in Cairo, perhaps the most famous Muslim university, provides such an education, and its scholars are, unsurprisingly, regarded by followers of Qutb with loathing and contempt. It is important to deprive those who fear scholarship in religion of social prestige and religious status. This is another reason why, incidentally, attacks on religion by those who think it is all blind and thoughtless provide support for the fundamentalists. For such attacks undermine the possibility of reflective theological thought as effectively as the diatribes of fundamentalists.

Third, a greater effort should be made to identify those

elements in religious systems that are liable to misuse, and to provide effective internal defences against such misuse. In the case of Islam, one could identify as potentially dangerous the belief that there is just one final and completely adequate source of truth, which is not subject to diverse human interpretations and that is capable of solving all human problems. There is the belief that unbelievers wilfully reject divine revelation and so are evil and expendable, sometimes even that there are particular enemies who can be blamed for all the wrongs of the world. And there is the rejection of freedom of conscience and belief (which must, of course, include the freedom to reject *Shari'a* as well as the rejection of belief in God and Muhammad).

In response to these dangers, Islam only needs to point to its own history to show that there are many diverse ways of interpreting *Shari'a*, and that no Muslim society has ever succeeded in eliminating all social problems, however dominant it has been. Human thought is diverse and corruptible, in religion or outside it. Muslims can admit this without conceding that the Qur'an itself is imperfect or fallible. But divine revelation needs to be carefully distinguished from human attempts to interpret and apply it. Islam is an extremely diverse and historically changing set of institutions, and it is an error – and a dangerous one – for either Muslims or non-Muslims to think of Islam as one monolithic socio-political system that requires no addition of knowledge from elsewhere.

Islam also needs to be careful not to demonise its opponents. Again all this requires is careful and detailed knowledge of those opponents. There are good reasons for not accepting the existence of God, and the history of philosophical thought lays them out pretty thoroughly. Unless you are going to regard philosophers like Kant and Hume as stupid or morally corrupt, you have to admit that the evidence for God and for a particular divine revelation is not overwhelming. Kant and Hume were both men of exemplary moral concern and character. Some of the most rational and morally committed individuals in history have not been religious, and the right of dissent is an important consequence of respecting other people and taking them seriously. Where there is respect for the freedom and beliefs of others, it is inevitable that any form of truly global society must permit many varieties of political and religious thought.

Islam should have no difficulty in making these things clear. The Qur'an itself allows for conscientious disagreement in religion, and enjoins that there should be no compulsion in religion. There is no reason why Islam should not invite all to share its vision of God and human destiny. But there is every reason why Islam and any other political or religious system should not compel others to adopt that vision.

Dangers of violence in Christianity

I have talked of Islam because among modern religious believers it is Islamic Jihadists who pose the greatest clear and present threat to the rest of the world. I am not pretending that there is any easy answer to threats of this sort. I have suggested that there are political issues of justice and gross inequality that need to be addressed. There is a pressing need for the extension of programmes of education, including education in global religious history, and especially in the complex relationships between political and social life and religious thought throughout the world (in the United States as well as in Saudi Arabia). A strengthening of traditional Islam, with its long scholarly legal tradition, and in its many varieties, is one of the best defences we have. But of course it is essential that traditional Islam does not remain isolated and cut off from the global issues of the day. Despite differences of language and culture, Islamic scholarship needs to enter into positive conversation with modern science and liberal thought, and with other global ideologies such as Christianity and humanism. Remaining true to its own basic revelation of

God, it can grow by being open to all the other resources of knowledge in God's world, and by seeking a joint way of addressing the major problems of human survival and well-being in the future.

Exactly the same sorts of comment apply to Christianity. There are potentially dangerous doctrines in Christianity too, and from time to time they have given rise to violence and warfare. There is no conceivable system of religious or political thought that has no potential dangers. The most we can do is to find the most adequate internal checks against those dangers being realised. But when economic and social affairs are in crisis, nothing on earth can prevent humans from misusing any system whatsoever.

In Christianity too there is an obvious need for clear and impartial teaching of the global history of religions and of political worldviews. Christians have tortured and killed people for having the 'wrong' beliefs, and that is because of the view that having correct beliefs, or belonging to the true church, is necessary for eternal salvation. Christians have regarded Jews as responsible for the death of Christ, and have discriminated against them. Christians have regarded infidels as 'enemies of God' and have fought against them, most spectacularly in the Crusades. And Christians have attempted to impose their beliefs on whole societies, repressing all other forms of worship.

These are occurrences that anyone with humane and liberal views would regard with horror. They are views that most contemporary Christians would regard with horror. There is no denying that they happened. There have been religious wars, religious persecutions and religious hatreds. They are inexcusable. But, especially perhaps in the Christian case, they stand in need of explanation. How could a faith which was almost, if not quite, pacifist in its origins, become a religion of warrior–knights and Inquisitors?

The pacifism is clear in the teachings of Jesus that say one should not resist evil or take revenge (the definitive text is the

Gospel of Matthew, chapters 5–7), and from the fact that he went to his death and did not take up arms against Roman military occupation. So what happened? There are many books dealing with this problem, and they should certainly be consulted before any easy answer is offered. The issue is as complex as any real historical question, and there is no one established answer among professional historians. But some things are fairly evident.

One is that human history as a whole is a history of warfare and violence. The early recorded history of humanity is a story of imperial conquests and wars. Assyria, Babylon, Persia, Egypt and Greece, together with almost endless waves of so-called barbarian hordes, make our books of early human history into chronicles of almost continual conquest and warfare.

Religion may have played some part in these affairs, but it is the desire for power and wealth that is the constant factor. It is natural that warrior–kings should try to enlist the loyalty of their followers by getting them to defend some preferred set of values, and to denigrate the values of other societies. Since religions usually embody values, kings can readily enlist the gods on their side, as protectors of the values of empire.

So it was with the Roman empire, whose gods favoured Roman conquests, Roman justice and Roman law, and treated the gods of other peoples with contempt. But these gods were employees of the emperor – indeed, soon the emperors joined them in person. The gods were projections of imperial values and ambitions, with all the ambiguity of empire.

This is not all that the gods were. The pagan gods, for most of their devotees, probably expressed the transcendent beauty of nature, the objective demands of social duty and of personal virtue, and sometimes the hope of deliverance from suffering and death. But the gods were many and diverse. There were gods of war, of destruction and of disease, as well as of love and of healing. It was easy for emperors to choose the gods that suited them best, and to enrol them in the service of imperial ambition. It was not the gods, or belief in the gods, that caused war. But once a war of conquest had begun, some gods at least proved useful in inspiring loyalty to the imperial cause.

In Rome, Mithras was a favourite god of the imperial legions, and rituals of bathing in bull's blood and endurance through trials, and the celebration of strength and courage and manly fellowship, made this a warrior religion that was well suited to the needs of the empire. Nevertheless, only a minority of soldiers followed the cult of Mithras. Most of them were in it for the pay, the honour or to avoid a worse fate. The vast imperial struggles of the ancient world were not wars of religion. They were wars of conquest, to impose imperial order and rule on areas that could provide the ruling elite with stupendous power, wealth and security.

Christianity and the Roman empire

The Christian God was not a god of empire, but a god of slaves and labourers, of the poor and oppressed in the insignificant Roman province of Judea. Jesus was not a very good example for warrior–kings – he had entered Jerusalem on a donkey, not a white charger, and had signally failed to challenge Roman imperialism at any point. The extraordinary thing is that by the time of the emperor Theodosius, in the fourth century CE, Christianity had become the official religion of the Roman empire.

The consequences were far-reaching. The new faith banned infanticide, encouraged the building of early hospitals and institutions for caring for the elderly and sick, and sought to outlaw capital punishment. It did have humanising effects on the empire. But the influence was not one way, and the church was gradually drawn into the life of the imperial court and its intrigues. In time, the senior bishops were largely drawn from the families of the court, and the imperial concern for order and uniformity throughout the empire led to the persecution of radicals and non-conformists.

In the eastern Byzantine empire, the emperors took a leading role in church affairs – Constantine himself is said to have had a hand in drafting the Creed of Nicea, which became the test of orthodoxy in the church. The concern for 'correct doctrine', for defining exactly what Christians ought to believe, and for condemning and excommunicating alternative views, developed in this context. Originally a set of fluid and diverse practices and beliefs, with varying relations to its parent-faith, Judaism, the Christian Church became increasingly concerned with orthodox belief and practice. A church hierarchy was established, mimicking that of the imperial court, and the creeds became ways of sorting out loyal and trustworthy supporters of the official, imperial, views from those whose radicalism might be a danger to the unity of the empire.

Such dangers were very real, because the Roman empire was in decay. In the East, the imperial army was defeated by Muslim invaders in 636 CE, and that began a long process of decline until at last the Byzantine empire ceased to exist with the fall of Constantinople in 1453. In the West, the empire was subject to constant invasion by barbarians, and ended much earlier, in the fifth century. As Augustine wrote his great work, *The City of God*, barbarians were besieging his city, Hippo, and were shortly to overrun it. This was an empire in crisis. Religious intrigues, controversies, and frantic attempts to preserve or impose unity at any cost, were reflections of imperial crises in the life of the imperial church.

As the Roman empire crumbled, two further major social factors affected the church. First, as various northern European warrior–tribes were assumed into the church, largely by conquest, they brought with them their warrior religions and baptised them, rather superficially in many cases, into the Christian faith. Thus Christ, however improbable it may seem, became a warrior–god, and one of the apostles, James (Sant Iago in Spain), appeared in visions with a bloody sword at the head of the armies of Christendom. Secondly, Muslim imperial expansion had become a serious threat to Europe. By 712 CE the Arabs and Moroccans (the Moors) had conquered North Africa and Spain, and later the empires of the Seljuk and Ottoman Turks invaded Europe, devastating Poland and laying siege to Vienna in 1529. These were campaigns of imperial conquest in the traditional manner, claiming power over and draining wealth from conquered territories. But since the aggressors were Muslim and the defenders were Christian, a potent religious dimension was added to the ethnic and nationalist dimensions.

The Crusades

This was the context in which the Crusades originated. The Crusades are sometimes thought of as aggressive Christian attacks on Muslim territory, or even on Islam itself. But it was Arab armies who had swept through the eastern Mediterranean lands and were engaged in attacks on the remnants of the Byzantine empire. In 1054 the Byzantines appealed to Pope Gregory VII for military aid against the Seljuk Turks, who had invaded Anatolia and massacred thousands of Christians, and were now threatening Constantinople itself. The First Crusade of 1096 was a result of this and other appeals from the Eastern empire, and it can thus quite reasonably be seen as an attempt to defend imperial territory against an aggressive invader.

It is, however, beyond dispute that the Crusades were a major disaster. In the Fourth Crusade Constantinople was conquered and pillaged, not by Muslims, but by Western Christians, who tried to erect a new Latin kingdom in the Holy Land rather than to defend Byzantium. Yet again desire for power, sheer greed and the malevolence of indiscriminate slaughter corrupted a possibly just intention into a series of morally evil and militarily disastrous adventures.

The Crusades can be seen as justified defence of the

Byzantine empire against Arab and Turkish invaders. But their conduct and continuance rapidly became unjustifiable on any Christian principles. That is because the use of force was indiscriminate and disproportionate, and the defence of Byzantium was quickly abandoned for the sake of acquiring private wealth, and the establishment of an unsustainable Latin empire.

The Crusades were not only against Muslims. There were Crusades against many forces considered to be threats to the Christian empire in the West, including Crusades against indigenous populations. The most infamous of these is probably the Crusade against the Albigenses in France. The Albigenses believed, among other things, that matter was evil, that Christ was not truly human and did not die on the cross, and that the church was doing the work of the devil. Naturally enough the Catholic Church saw this as a threat, and after the Albigenses assassinated a papal legate in 1208, Pope Innocent authorised a Crusade against them. The affair turned into a war between northern and southern French forces (many of the southerners being Catholics), and ended with the incorporation of Languedoc into the French monarchical realm. There was a strong political dimension to this struggle, but the Catholic Church did condone the use of force on religious grounds, and the Inquisition arose as a continuation of the policy of eradicating heresy by force. Such a policy now seems almost incomprehensible to most Christians, as well as to most secular liberals, and it needs an effort of historical imagination to gain any comprehension of it.

Religion and types of social order

In assessing this situation, we need to remember that all societies claim the right to defend their order and security and way of life against attack, whether that attack comes from within or without. If, for instance, an elected leader takes dictatorial powers and closes down democratic institutions, it would be widely thought to be justifiable to eliminate that leader, as he is attacking democracy. Or if monarchy is forcibly abolished by a revolutionary party, many would think it justifiable to respond with force to restore it. Such actions might only be justifiable if the order attacked has a clear mandate from the people, if they have a good chance of success, and if the harm they will cause is likely to be a good deal less than the harm caused by lack of action.

Using these principles, we can see how in a country where Catholicism (or Islam or secular democracy) has wide approbation, and is liable to be unjustly overthrown or imperilled, the state might be justified in protecting the system against such a threat by some use of force. It should be noted that in formulating this position, I have assumed that the approbation of the people in general is an important consideration. This is to assume a generally democratic position, that government should broadly express the will of the majority. In many democracies, it is understood that in addition the rights of minorities that do not threaten positive harm to society should be tolerated. It follows that only those views of the majority that do not imperil the rights of minorities should be protected by the threat of force.

In non-democratic societies, however, appeal to the views of the majority, even with the addition of toleration of non-harmful minorities, might not be considered morally overriding. It might be thought that the ruling elite knows best what is good for society. Ordinary people need to be educated to know what is best for them; they need to follow a strong lead; and they need to be protected from misleading influences. Of course rulers should not simply oppress populations. But neither should they bow to the wishes of the majority, whatever they are. Rulers should aim at the good of their people, and that certainly includes aiming at their general health and security. This might mean having laws such as banning smoking in public places, and implementing that ban by force (by fine or imprisonment). There is a difference between tyrannical governments and paternalistic governments, in that the latter have a concern for the public good, though they do not accept that the public good is best established by majority vote.

Such was, broadly speaking, the official view of the Catholic Church before the Second Vatican Council of the 1960s. The church was charged with the duty of caring for the souls of the people and instructing them in their moral and spiritual duties. Any undermining of this obligation would be morally and spiritually dangerous. So it could be opposed by the threat of force.

The crucial questions are whether heretical groups like the Albigenses did pose a threat to the good order of society and to the souls of men and women, and whether that threat was justly punishable by torture and death. It may seem to us that people should be free in matters of personal belief, as long as that does not do evident physical or mental harm to others. And even if it did, the perpetrators should be treated humanely, not killed.

I entirely agree, and it is demonstrable that Christianity as understood in the New Testament entails exactly these principles. For the first Christians were dissenters in Jewish and Roman society, and they would have to agree that it was wrong for the Romans to persecute and torture them. If consistent, they would then have to agree that it is in general wrong to persecute people for religious dissent (though consistency is not always very apparent in human affairs).

Nevertheless, one has to admit, as a matter of historical record, that the Romans tortured and killed Christians for refusing to worship Caesar as god. Such heterodox beliefs were thought to undermine the state, and death was considered a suitable punishment. A thousand years later, Christians, now allied by birth and social structure with ruling political powers who were just as violent as the Romans had ever been, and who felt desperately threatened without and within, fell into the same panic-stricken modes of thought. They victimised those within their own societies who did not conform – particularly Jews and unbelievers. They blessed the warriors who went out to defend the tottering boundaries of Christendom. And they consolidated a strongly disciplined hierarchical structure of the church as a defence against the radical and barbarian voices that threatened the last remnants of classical civilisation that the church precariously preserved.

There are certainly some major historical blots on the record of the Christian churches. I have suggested that they were due to three main factors: the church's involvement with the violent political powers of the dying Roman empire, faced with invading barbarians and Muslims who placed that empire under a clear and pressing threat; an ideology of illiberal paternalism; and that factor which is never completely absent from any human affairs and institutions: sin, or hatred, greed and envy.

At the same time the church did preserve ancient classical culture in times of chaos and anarchy. It inspired the building of great cathedrals and sublime works of art, in icons, mosaics and illuminated manuscripts. In its monasteries it gave rise to traditions of scholarship and philosophical debate, as well as helping to build a sound agricultural economy and a refuge for those seeking a sense of the presence of God. And in ordinary life it campaigned for hospitality for strangers, care for the sick, education for all, and the preaching of love, compassion and hope in a world darkened by plague, disease, the cruelty of war, and early death. These quotidian mercies are hugely positive factors that are largely hidden from the eyes of those historians who notice only the grand movements of the rich and powerful. But they are where we might expect to find the most positive fruits of a religion that has always claimed to speak most of all to the poor and everyday, and to let its works of charity be performed in secret, silently.

What, then, are the best ways of counteracting the three main dangers I have mentioned? The first would be to dissociate the church from imperialist centres of power, and return it to the dispossessed and the poor of the earth – in modern parlance, to the Third World rather than to Western corridors of power. The second would be for the church to renounce illiberal paternalism, and wholeheartedly accept freedom of religion, of conscience and of dissent. The third would be, not to eradicate sin, which is impossible, but to be more aware of social structures – in the church as well as in society in general – that encourage tendencies to pride, greed and hatred, and to try to put in place structures that do not reward such tendencies, but instead encourage humility, altruism and compassion.

The Christian churches have attempted to do this in modern times. The Second Vatican Council in the 1960s, for example, affirmed freedom of conscience and religion. But there is undoubtedly more that could be done to disentangle religion more clearly from illiberal and violent political systems, and allow it to concentrate on its own distinctive role of articulating human reverence for and positive relationship with the Supreme Good.

Religious wars

No one would deny that there have been religious wars in human history. Catholics have fought Protestants, Sunni Muslims have fought Shi'a Muslims, and Hindus have fought Muslims.

However, no one who has studied history could deny that most wars in human history have not been religious. And in the case of those that have been religious, the religious component has usually been associated with some non-religious, social, ethnic or political component that has exerted a powerful influence on the conflicts.

To find examples of non-religious wars we need look no further than the first half of the twentieth century, in which more people were killed in war than in the whole of the rest of human history. The two world wars were not fought on religious grounds at all. The reasons for them are complex, but they largely involve the desire for territory, national pride and the aspiration to extend imperial control. Where religion was appealed to in support of the war – as it was in the First World War in both Germany and England and France – it was the same religion and the same God who was called on for support on both sides. Religion was called up in support of national duty, or what was believed to be national duty. But there were no religious doctrines or practices at issue in those wars. The most terrible conflicts in human history were not religious.

Not only that, but in the first half of the twentieth century Communist, explicitly anti-religious, policies were responsible for millions of deaths in their own countries. It is estimated that in the USSR, 20 million people were killed, in China 65 million, in North Korea 2 million, and in Cambodia 2 million – all by Communist governments exterminating their own populations. These were politically motivated exterminations; religion was not a major factor.

The terrifying record of human oppression continues into the twenty-first century. A report from the UN Commissioner for Refugees in 2006 – *The State of the World's Refugees: Human Displacement in the New Millennium*[2] – estimates that there are now 25 million internally displaced persons in the world. These are people who have been driven from their homes by the governments of their own states, for political, economic and environmental reasons.

Countries with significant numbers of internally displaced persons in January 2005 included: Serbia and Montenegro, Croatia, Bosnia and Herzegovina, Georgia, Azerbaijan, Russia, Afghanistan, Burma, Sri Lanka, Burundi, Sudan, Angola, Ivory Coast, Liberia and Colombia. In the Democratic Republic of Congo and Sudan alone there were 7.5 million refugees in 2005. In Somalia (a state with one religion and ethnicity, though divided into four main clans) 400,000 people have been displaced from their homes and livelihoods, and live in shacks, while the country is torn apart by warlords and their militias. In Burma, where the whole population is officially Buddhist, the Karen National Union and other minority ethnic groups have been fighting for ethnic homelands against the military dictatorship since 1962. An estimated 1 million Karens have fled the country, and 2 million now live under conditions of forced labour and extortion – that is almost half the Karen population. In Uganda, a country that is 85 per cent Christian, a rebel group called 'The Lord's Resistance Army' has committed appalling atrocities. But despite the fact that the leader of this 'army', Joseph Kony, claims to be a spirit medium with his own idiosyncratic version of Christianity, this is not a religious struggle. There are no issues of religious belief at stake. Its basis is ethnic and tribal.

The International Institute for Strategic Studies is probably the most reliable source for statistics on war. In its 2006 report on the military balance in the world[3], it focuses attention on four major areas of violence or potential military threat: Iran, Iraq and Afghanistan, North Korea and China. There is no religious dimension to the latter two, and the Iranian threat is more to do with the alleged desire of Iran to possess nuclear weapons than with any religious consideration. The conflicts in Iraq and Afghanistan have strong religious dimensions, but the report picks out 'ethnicity, identity, power struggles, resources, inequality and oppression' as the root causes of violence, with religion being used in support where possible. It should be kept in mind that the wars in Iraq and Afghanistan were initiated by major imperial powers (the USA and Russia, respectively), which wished either to overthrow a dictatorship or to impose imperial rule. Religion became an important factor as a response to a perceived but non-religious threat. Moreover, the Institute's report names over 260 armed non-state groups, only a minority of which have a religious component. And it calls attention to the huge increase in military privatisation – mercenary groups, with 30,000 personnel in Iraq alone. These groups do not exist for any religious motive.

So, although religion can play a part in violent conflict, and though many Western media seem obsessed with religious threats, detailed surveys show that genuinely religious wars are few, that much of the violence in the modern world has nothing to do with religion, and that where religion is a factor, it is called on in support of other grievances that seem in most cases to be the precipitating causes of conflict.

The list of atrocities and human tragedies is long and immensely depressing. If you set alongside it the number of violent conflicts that are religious in origin, religious wars are a tiny minority of human conflicts. War and violence seem to be part of the human condition. To see religion even as a main cause of this is simply to miss the real problem, and therefore to give up all hope of finding any solution. Even in those cases where religion is a major factor, there is more hope of understanding the situation when other economic or ethnic factors are taken into account.

For example, the English Civil War of the seventeenth century did have a strong religious component in the Puritanism of Oliver Cromwell. But to understand how the monarchy came to be overthrown we need to appreciate the political conflict between crown and parliament, the intransigence of King Charles I, the desire of the landowning classes for greater political power, and the grievances of the disenfranchised population. Religious considerations had to fuse with all these factors to produce the English revolution. A 'one cause only' analysis of the situation is vastly over-simple and very unhelpful. In this case, religious views were important in bonding together Cromwell's 'New Model Army'. But they needed a context in which there were significant social discontents and political opportunities that the Puritan religious party could use to popularise their beliefs and make them socially relevant.

Also in the seventeenth century, the Thirty Years' War in Europe between Protestants and Catholics could plausibly be seen as a religious war. It began in 1618, when the rulers of Prague were overthrown by Bohemian rebels. It ended in 1648 with the Peace of Westphalia, which guaranteed the independence of the Netherlands, the German states and the Swiss cantons, and the ceding of Alsace to France. This was a war between Protestants and Catholics, but it was also a war against traditional Catholic imperial powers on behalf of rising forces of national independence. The German princes rebelled against the authority of the Habsburg (Holy Roman) empire, and Spain fought for its imperial control of the Netherlands. The war devastated central Europe, and involved massacres on a large scale. All this must be seen in the wider context of battles between France, England, Spain and Austria, many of which did not carry a religious dimension, but were about imperial control or new nationalistic aspirations. The Catholic countries of Austria, Spain and France were just as capable of fighting each other as they were of fighting Protestants. Here again, then, religion played a part, but wider factors of nationalism and political authority were more widespread and important.

A sociological analysis

The British sociologist David Martin considers the issue of war and religion in his book *Does Christianity Cause War?*[4]. The book provides a detailed and subtle analysis of the sociological factors involved in warfare and social violence, and shows how very diverse and complex those factors are. He draws a distinction between differentiated and undifferentiated forms of religion. The former makes a clear distinction between religion and other aspects of social and political life, whereas the latter does not. In the Byzantine empire, for example, religion was integrated into the political structure of the state, so that the emperor was also a religious leader, and religious and political life were closely intertwined. This is still true in some contemporary societies – Martin instances Serbian Orthodoxy and Croatian Catholicism. But since the eighteenth century there has been an increasing social differentiation of religion from state authority, and religious belief has become a more voluntary and pluralist phenomenon.

Religion, like ethnicity or language, a sense of historical continuity or a distinctive culture, is a marker of identity, and, he says, such 'markers of identity, whatever they are, provide *in special definable circumstances* the preconditions of conflict'. Religion is one marker of identity among others, and whether or not it becomes a socially significant one depends upon the social conditions at the time.

Thus when a nation starts to differentiate itself from religious views, but retains a positive relationship with the majority religion within its territory where minority religions also exist, 'conflict is likely where the minority religion is found among an ethnic and/or linguistic group which occupies a peripheral territory, which has a sizeable power base, and can call upon allies across the border'.

So religion, as a marker of identity, can play a role in violent social conflicts. The case of Serbia, a new nation carved out of a collapsing repressive Communist empire, and feeling itself surrounded by enemies, is a case where Orthodoxy is used as a major marker.

Other markers are usually more important, however – as in Quebec, where linguistic and cultural factors predominate. Professor Martin writes, 'I know of no evidence to show that the absence of a religious factor in the contention of rival identities and incompatible claims leads to a diminution in the degree of enmity and ferocity.'

The argument is that religion can get drawn into the political realm where force is often used. But in fact 'religion and the power of religion deal primarily in a personal mode, whatever overlaps there may be with power in the political sphere'. That is, religion deals primarily with individual relation to the Spiritual Ultimate. And to the extent that religion becomes fully differentiated from the nation state, religion often becomes a positive force for peace and reconciliation.

What this shows is that religious beliefs in themselves are not causes of violence. It is when religious institutions are blended with political institutions that religion can be enlisted in the use of force – and even then it is just one identity-marker among others, varying in its importance from one context to another.

Can religion be a force for peace?

Professor Martin's discussion is about Christianity, and it could be claimed that Islam is an inherently more political religion, perhaps not capable of fully undergoing social differentiation from the nation state. That is indeed part of the rhetoric of modern militant Islam. But examination of the role that Muslim religious leaders play in actual Muslim countries shows that this is indeed rhetoric, in the sense of being an unrealised dream.

Generally speaking, in most Muslim countries there is an agreement that government legislation will not contradict *Shari'a*, in one of its interpretations. But most economic and political decisions are made by secular rulers, and the reality is that Christianity is as influential on the government of the United States – an officially secular country – as Islam is on the government of Egypt – an officially Muslim country. That is just what Islamic militants complain about. But it should not be thought that they represent Islam as a whole, or more than a tiny minority view.

The traditional Muslim view of *jihad*, of a justifiable use of violence, is in fact very similar to the traditional Catholic 'just war' tradition. In both cases the voice of religion opposes the use of indiscriminate violence and insists on the objectivity of moral rules that curb the expression of desires. It is a corrupted view of religion, influenced by alien secular political doctrines, that supports terror. In specific societies, religious leaders tend to follow the national line – as we see from the attitudes of religious leaders in the First and Second World Wars. But religious views tend to moderate and restrict the use of violence. If religion is dangerous in this area, it is because it undermines the use of violence in defence of national interests, not because it motivates violence.

This discussion shows that detailed historical and sociological analysis makes generalisations almost impossible. The same set of beliefs can give rise to quite different consequences in different social circumstances. The same beliefs can even be interpreted in quite different ways by different societies.

In addition, the attitudes of religious believers are themselves quite complex. Broadly speaking, nominal believers are more likely to adopt intolerant and divisive attitudes than committed believers, while a good number of believers (though a minority) are prominent in counselling peace and reconciliation – and are often likely to be murdered for their pains. Religion can be a factor that intensifies conflicts, though it is also a factor in bringing about the cessation of conflict. Religion takes on the complexion of its social environment, and the influence it has depends largely on other forces in that environment.

As I look at the evidence, it seems to me that the teachings of religion are wholeheartedly adopted only by a minority of religious adherents, and that they usually adopt an overt attitude of seeking justice and peace. But the realities of political situations are such that religious institutions can be used by authorities to support their own cause, and the rhetoric of religion can then be used to enlist loyalty to very ambiguous policies, for which the use of violence can seem to be (and, if we are honest, for most of us sometimes is) justified.

It is in such terms that we should see the modern proliferation of Islamic terrorist groups. There are many terrorist groups in the modern world. Some are left-wing or Maoist; some are right-wing or Nationalist; some are ethnic; some are nationalistic; but quite a large number of active groups are 'religious'. If we deduct the religious groups, there are still plenty of terrorists groups left, so it is obvious that religion is not the only cause of terrorism. The large number of Islamic terrorist groups is quite clearly connected with the Israeli-Palestinian conflict. Considering that Israel is officially a secular state and that most Zionists were not 'religious' Jews, this turns out to be largely a conflict about perceived injustice, a fight for territorial sovereignty, and a clash of cultures between broadly 'Western' and 'non-Western' ways of life. Religion certainly fuels the conflict, mostly on the Islamic side, but the root causes are social and political. It is important for religious groups to become more aware of their potential to be used as markers of identity that inflame conflict situations. They need to find ways of encouraging the more central religious tendencies that make for peace and reconciliation.

Religion cannot be exempted from the almost universal human tendency towards hatred of and violence against others. But it is historically incorrect to say that most violent conflicts have religion as their cause, or that the worst cases of violence are religious. That distinction must go to ethnic and tribal conflicts in modern Africa, or to Communist and Fascist pogroms in the twentieth century. Religion has been implicated in violence, especially where it becomes a marker of identity in situations of social conflict. But religion has often been a voice of moderation and reconciliation, and that is its true role, as the scriptural documents of all the great world religions clearly state. Without religion, the historical evidence clearly shows, there would still be wars and violence on earth.

With it, there is at least a chance that the voice of those who give their lives for no apparent earthly benefit but just for the sake of good alone may be heard with greater clarity. With religion there is a chance that, at least in places, for a while, and to some extent, goodness may flourish on the earth.

Part Two
Are religious beliefs irrational?

Chapter 4
Faith and reason

Basic beliefs

The historical evidence is that religion is not the major cause of violence in the world. So though it can be dangerous when – usually against its own most deeply rooted principles – it incites to hatred and intolerance, it is not a major cause of unjustified physical conflict. But some would argue that religious belief is dangerous in another way. It is dangerous simply because it is an irrational form of belief. Religion is a danger to truth and to rationality, and it replaces thoughtful concern for facts with blind acceptance on authority of absurd beliefs. This is a form of intellectual harm.

In assessing this claim, we need to ask whether religious beliefs are, as such, irrational, blind and clearly false. Can there be such a thing as reasonable religious belief? A blunt response is that there evidently are reasonably held religious beliefs. Are we to accuse Anselm, Aquinas, Kant, Kierkegaard, Hegel, Descartes and Leibniz of being irrational? If we do so, we are setting the standard of rationality impossibly high. These people define what we call reasonableness.

Some critics of religion think that the only reasonable beliefs are those that can be confirmed by the methods of science, by public observation, measurement and experiment. The trouble with that statement is that it is self-refuting. It is not itself confirmable by observation and experiment. So, according to its own criterion of reasonableness, it cannot be reasonable. This is admittedly a very short argument. But it has the advantage of being absolutely conclusive. If only scientifically testable statements are reasonable, then this statement (that 'only scientifically testable statements are reasonable') is not reasonable. Conversely, if this statement *is* reasonable, then some statements are reasonable that are not scientifically testable. So the statement is either unreasonable or false.

Many of the most important beliefs we have in life are not scientifically testable, but we still live our whole lives by them. I have beliefs about what happened in history, about whether my partner loves me or not, about what sorts of acts are morally right, about what sorts of music are of the greatest worth, about what political policies we should adopt, about whether I can trust my friends. There are thousands of things I believe that are not scientifically testable. Quite a lot of them, I hope, are reasonable – though some may be based on ignorance or prejudice.

I cannot think of any general rule that would tell me just what makes a belief reasonable, or such that I can justifiably hold it. But I know that some of my beliefs are so basic to my life that they are the keystones of my whole outlook on life. If they collapsed, I would be a different person. I have no real evidence for them, but they are foundational to how I think and act. Examples would be: there is some explanation, whether scientific or not, for every event that happens (things do not happen for no reason). Human beings are basically good and well-meaning, but they are also subject to terrible corruptions of greed, hatred and ignorance. People ought to consider the welfare of others, and ideally of all other sentient beings, at least to some extent. And I would add: it is appropriate to feel awe and reverence at the beauty and complexity of nature, to feel gratitude for the fact of existence, and to sense the presence of some sort of transcendent power and value in moments of understanding truth, appreciating beauty and enjoying friendship.

These are unevidenced basic beliefs, beliefs by which we live (most of us), and which are so basic that there are no other beliefs on which they could be based, or from which they could be inferred. We do not get them by observation. Perhaps we should just say these are beliefs that are conditions of the possibility of living and acting in the world as we do. They provide our basic perspective on existence. If they have reasons, those reasons lie in the coherence and integration they bring to all the varied sorts of experience and knowledge that we have.

Three worldviews

Everybody has some basic worldview, even if they would not give their beliefs such a grand title. A worldview is a set of concepts for interpreting experience. It is possible to have a common sense worldview. This would just say that things are as they appear to us. We live in a world of coloured solid objects and we find out what is real by seeing, touching, smelling or tasting things. This is a pretty naive view, and it collapses as soon as we know about the scientific finding that colour and solidity are how objects appear to our senses, while the underlying reality is very different. It could be atoms or sub-atomic particles. It could be something even stranger, like superstrings in eleven dimensions. Whatever it is, reality is not what it seems to the senses, and we do not find out what is real just by seeing and touching things at all.

A different worldview that owes more to modern science is the materialist worldview. For this view, reality is what science, especially physics, says it is. We discover what is real by experiment, certainly, but we would not even be able to devise and understand experiments in quantum physics unless we had a great deal of mathematical ability and a great deal of theory, which we accept basically because of its elegance and predictive power. Materialism is the view that reality is whatever science says it is, and our means of access to it is by highly sophisticated abstract theories, by means of theorising, and not just, as in common sense, by means of the senses.

The appeal of materialism is that it is a fairly simple theory, reducing reality to just one sort of stuff – matter, energy or superstrings, perhaps. It fits well with the fact that scientific theorising works, and produces amazingly acute predictions. And if we think that human existence seems unplanned, accidental, even cruel and pointless, it provides a theory that confirms those thoughts, and tells us there is no purpose or plan in human existence. There is just the inexorable rule of law, and the blind and purposeless circulation of sub-atomic particles, sometimes giving rise to an illusory appearance of design or intelligence.

However, there are also major problems with materialism. The most obvious is that quantum physics seems to dissolve the idea of matter entirely. Whatever the strange hidden basis of quantum theory is, it is not hard lumps of solid stuff. Electrons become probability waves in Hilbert space, matter is just one form of energy, and we do not know all the other forms there may be.

There are basic problems with theories in modern physics. It is, for instance, very difficult to make quantum theory consistent with relativity theory, and the well-established quantum property of non-locality does not seem to fit with relativity physics as we know it. It looks as though we do not have a very good grasp of the basis even of physical reality.

In addition, consciousness and the contents of consciousness – especially mathematics, logic, feelings and intentions – resist translation into purely physical terms. To most of us it is obvious that we need to explain many aspects of human life in terms of intentions, goals and evaluations. But all such things simply disappear in materialism. The simplicity that materialism offers may be bought at the cost of overlooking the real complexity that is part of reality. And of course if we believe that there is a spiritual dimension to reality, that in seeking truth, beauty and goodness we are seeking things that really exist, and that it is possible to apprehend a transcendent personal reality of more than human value and power, then materialism will not match our experience at all.

So a third main worldview is that of idealism. This view states that the fundamental character of reality is that of consciousness or mind. The whole material world is an appearance of what is fundamentally a complex mental reality. Consciousness is not just a by-product of the material brain, as materialists think. On the contrary, the brain and body are appearances, material forms, of an underlying mental reality. The material world exists in order to let finite forms of mind grow, relate to one another as objects in a common world, and develop their own attitudes and personalities from the store of potentialities and capacities that their material environment provides. Idealism, too, has the virtue of simplicity, of finding one unitary type of reality as the basis of all the complexity we see around us. It is able to take full account of the existence and importance of human awareness, feelings and uniquely personal experiences. And it encourages us to see purpose and wisdom in the existence of the natural world, providing a basis for spiritual experiences and beliefs, without reducing them to illusions.

These are just three worldviews that exist and are very widely held in our world. There are many others. Christian theism is one of those others, since it agrees with idealism that one personal conscious reality – God is primary, and is the basis of all material reality. But it agrees with materialism that the material world has its own proper reality, though it is ultimately dependent on God.

The contestability of worldviews

In general, what we call religious views tend towards idealism. There are hardly any materialist or purely common sense religions. But there are many interpretations of idealism, and many ways in which it may be qualified. So Buddhism, Hinduism, Confucianism and the Abrahamic faiths all take rather different interpretations of idealism. But they all hold that the spiritual dimension of human existence is the truly important dimension, and that the goal of religion is to make people aware of that dimension and enrich their lives by such awareness.

Many attacks on religion are based on the belief that idealism is false. There is no spiritual dimension to reality. The religious goal is unobtainable, based on a false view of reality, and illusory. It is therefore intellectual dishonesty to teach religious views as if they were true.

To make matters worse, thinkers like Richard Dawkins hold that, while materialism is based on painstaking research and rational thought, religious views are based on 'blind faith', some sort of leap in the dark, and so are plainly irrational and unthinking. Since ignorance is morally reprehensible, religious belief is not only based on falsehood and deceit, it is morally wrong.

What are we to say about this? Has Dawkins never read any philosophy? Is he not aware of the weaknesses of materialism? Is he not aware that the philosophy of common sense espoused by his favourite philosopher, David Hume, has been pretty comprehensively undermined by science? Or that Hume himself could never reconcile his commitment to sceptical reasoning, which undermined belief in causal laws and other persons as well as God, with his common sense beliefs? Does he really think that Descartes, Leibniz, Spinoza, Kant and Hegel were all unthinking simpletons? I believe that any reasonable person, faced with all the wide array of philosophical arguments throughout history and today, would be forced to admit that no worldview (no system of metaphysics) has gained universal consent among the informed peer group of professional philosophers.

Fashions come and go in philosophy, of course. In the first decades of the twentieth century, idealism was almost taken for granted among English-speaking philosophers. That was basically because they took as their start human conscious experience, and never dreamt of denying its very existence. In the latter half of the twentieth century, some of the very best professional philosophers opted for materialism. But most of them would concede that their view is provocative, and that there are deep and unresolved puzzles arising from quantum physics, from the existence of consciousness, and from the apparent irreducibility of historical, ethical, political and personal explanations to purely physical forms of explanation. Materialism is a bold and counterintuitive worldview – but that makes it all the more attractive to good philosophers. I have taught philosophy professionally in British universities for at least twenty years and am on the committee of the Royal Institute of Philosophy. Looking around at my philosopher colleagues in Britain, virtually all of whom I know at least from their published work, I would say that very few of them are materialists. Some – a minority probably – are idealists. A good number are theists. And most seem to be generally sceptical or agnostic about all worldviews, preferring to deal with specific tricky problems case by case, and to eschew general theories, materialism and idealism alike.

The point is that religious views are underpinned by highly sophisticated philosophical arguments. They are not blind leaps in the dark, and they are not based on unthinking acceptance of the assertions of some holy book. All such views are highly contested. None of them is universally accepted, or can even claim an overwhelming majority among philosophers. Systems of idealism cannot be strictly 'proved' to everyone's satisfaction. But neither can systems of materialism. These are ultimate, highly reasoned choices, none of which is obviously false or obviously true either.

The legend of the leap of faith

There is a particular view of the history of European philosophy that has almost become standard, but which is a misleading myth. That is that everybody used to accept that there were 'proofs of God'. The first cause argument (the universe must have a first cause) and the argument from design (design in the universe shows that there must be a designer) were supposed to prove that there must be a God. But then along came Immanuel Kant, who disproved all these proofs. After that, belief in God had no rational basis and had to become a rationally unjustifiable leap of faith (where 'faith' means belief without any evidence).

This view of the history of philosophy is skewed in a number of ways. First of all, it was never generally thought that, by starting only with the observable facts of the physical world, anyone could demonstrate that there has to be an intelligent first cause outside the universe. That would make God little more than an inference from observed facts, an absentee creator who was never actually present or experienced.

As a matter of historical fact, the main philosophical arguments derived largely from Plato and Aristotle, whose concern was not with some sort of inference from observed reality to something else. It was with the question of what the nature and character of observed reality was. In Plato's case, his arguments (or many of them) were intended to show that the observed world can be seen by reflective enquiry to be a world of appearances. The underlying reality can be known by the mind, by intellectual investigation, and ultimately by a vision of the Good, as the true reality of which the material world is an appearance. Philosophical argument was basically 'dialectic' – the presentation and re-presentation of limited perspectives on the world that might lead to distinguishing reality from appearance, and discerning that the inner character of reality is mental or spiritual. Plato does not ask us to infer an unseen designer. He tries to get us, through intense reflective argument, to see the world as the appearance, the manifestation, of a deeper spiritual reality that is akin to human consciousness, but of purer and more perfect goodness and beauty.

When Immanuel Kant came along, he did set out to undermine a specific set of rationalist arguments propounded by the philosophers Gottfried Leibniz and Christian Wolff. He did say that he set out to undermine knowledge in order to make room for 'faith'. But his whole critical philosophy was written as an attempt to set faith on a firm intellectual foundation, not to offer it as an alternative to intellectual thought.

A central part of Kant's philosophy was the attempt to show that reason leads to unavoidable contradictions when it tries to take observed reality as the true reality, as reality-in-itself. Only when you have, in this way, pushed reason to its limits can you see that reality must be something more than the empirical and observable, more than the world of Newtonian physics.

Faith, for Kant, was practical commitment made in areas where theoretical knowledge is impossible, but where there is still a pressure to make a rational choice. To make his case, he had to show that reason has its limits, and that it is necessary to make reasonable decisions in areas that go beyond those limits. For him, faith – faith in God, in moral freedom, and in the possibility of moral fulfilment ('happiness in accordance with virtue') – is supremely reasonable. It is not a leap in the dark. It is the use of reason beyond the limits of empirical verification.

Kant was, in fact, not so far from Plato. Kant did not speak of a vision of the Good because he was very suspicious, unduly suspicious perhaps, of claims to personal experience of God. But Kant did say that it was not optional but absolutely necessary to posit a rational and moral basis of the world, to posit the existence of the Supreme Good.

For Kant, all ultimate worldviews (all systems of transcendent metaphysics, as he would have said) are unverifiable. Yet it is supremely reasonable to have one, for we must base our practical life-commitments on something, on the best we can manage as human beings. That best, for Kant, was the postulate of a supremely good and wise God, on whom the rationality of the world and of human thought, and the reasonableness and obligatoriness of morality, could be founded. We have to go beyond the evidence, for reason itself compels us to do so.

You might say that it is deeply rational to have an ultimate worldview, but the fundamental beliefs of such a view cannot be based on any more basic evidence, for there is nothing more basic. How then can we choose? For Kant, we must choose the view that best supports our basic belief in the importance of reason, truth, and objective standards of beauty and goodness. This is a reasonable faith, but it is founded on a serious moral commitment that it is logically possible to reject.

So the history of European philosophy is not really a story of moving from proofs of God to irrational faith. It is rather a story of a clarification of the methods and limits of science (which Plato was unclear about, and Aristotle was partly wrong about), and of the basis of our most general worldviews in the sorts of practical commitment, the ways of life and moral orientation, that make possible distinctive human activities like science, morality and religion.

Whatever all this is, it is not the ending of rational thought by blind acceptance of some absolute authority. When Kant spoke of faith, he was absolutely not thinking of blind acceptance of authority. He called that 'heteronomy', subjecting your will to the will of another. In its place he called for 'autonomy' – daring to think for yourself, even about matters said to be revealed by God. Faith was in human reason and goodness, seen as founded on an ultimate reason and goodness, rooted in the nature of things.

Reason and revelation

Kant did not have much time for special revelation. But if you think the universe is founded on a supreme wisdom, beauty and goodness, it is very natural to suppose that at some specific points the character of that goodness and of the purposes it may have for the cosmos may become clearer. It is very reasonable to suppose that a being of supreme goodness would not leave humans completely in the dark about what they are meant to be and do, and about the nature of the Supreme Good itself. In a word, it is very reasonable to expect some sort of revelation of the character and purposes of God.

It is for this reason that it is wholly reasonable to think that some revelation of God has occurred in human history. That revelation will not overturn or contradict reason (except where reason is being misused). It will take human knowledge of God beyond what reason alone can establish. For most religious believers, God is not just a postulate of reason, as God was for Kant. God is one who makes the divine reality known in history and experience.

Reason and morality must still operate here, in asking what sort of revelations are reasonable and good, and which are truly irrational and morally flawed. But the interaction of reason and revelation is a two-way process – or better, a sort of spiralling from one pole (reason) to the other (revelation) and back again, seeking the balance of reasonable revelation. So in the history of Christianity there have been many Christians who have claimed special revelations from God, in dreams or visionary experiences. We have to ask whether such revelations are consistent with what we already believe of God, and with the sort of goodness we believe God has. If they contradict belief in the love of God revealed in Jesus – if, for example, they call us to kill other people – we should reject claims to revelation. But if they can be seen as developments from prior beliefs – new insights, perhaps, into the way in which slavery is in tension with love of your neighbour as yourself, or insights into the place and role of women – we may say that revelation has brought us to revise our existing moral beliefs.

So in prayer and in the experience of the church there can be new revelations of God's will. But they must be tested by their consonance with what is believed to be a definitive revelation of God, and by their coherence with the knowledge we have of the world from other sources. Revelation can expand the insights of reason, but reason must always test claims to revelation. That is why revelation is never static. It is always developing, though the limits of such development are set down by the original paradigm, in the case of Christianity, of Jesus and the Bible, the witness to his life and work.

Religion, then, is based on a worldview at least as reasonable as any other. Such worldviews cannot be based on evidence, for they determine what is going to count as evidence, and how evidence is going to be interpreted.

What makes worldviews reasonable?

There are fairly clear criteria for what makes acceptance of a worldview reasonable. There are rational procedures for setting out and defending a worldview. These procedures fall into three main groups:

+ First, it is desirable to aim at clarity and precision in stating the beliefs that are involved in a worldview. Such beliefs should ideally be arranged in order of logical dependence, so that one can tell which are the truly basic beliefs, how they relate to one another, and how other beliefs are derived from them.
+ Second, at each stage, alternatives to proposed beliefs should be identified and considered. Comparison with other worldviews is vital to forming a considered assessment of the weak and strong points of a worldview.
+ Third, it is necessary to test the adequacy of the worldview to the widest range of data, whether they are experiences

or other beliefs. The beliefs must be consistent with one another. The scheme should be as simple as possible – though it is obvious that the criteria of adequacy and simplicity may often contrast with one another, and a choice will have to be made between them in many cases. It would be unreasonable to adopt a very simple scheme that did not adequately cover all the various sorts of data that are available. The scheme should be coherent with all other knowledge. It should integrate data in an elegant, or patterned, way, so that the parts fit harmoniously into a convincing overall interpretation. Finally, the scheme should have creative power, generating new insights, approaches or paradigms, enabling data to be organised in new and more illuminating ways.

In applying these criteria, there is an important and ineliminable element of personal judgment involved. They are not rules to be applied separately and automatically. They are criteria to be balanced against each other and woven into a convincing narrative. As in all historical, legal and political judgments, rationality consists in assembling the largest array of relevant data, organising them in a clarifying manner, and in a way that is fruitful for suggesting further advances in knowledge.

In the end, all reason can do is require that these procedures are followed. It cannot dictate one agreed result, for that will depend on differing emphases laid on differing data, different organising paradigms that seem to illuminate the complexity of experience, and differing practical commitments that express basic judgments about what is important in life. Religious worldviews are not rational because they produce overwhelming arguments that 'prove' the truth of the worldview to all competent people. They are rational because they are structured and elaborated in a critical and reflective way, using rational criteria for judgment that are always open to diverse interpretations.

In a sense, each worldview embodies a large element of judgment and faith, and there is no way of avoiding that. Religious worldviews can therefore be, and often are, as reasonable as non-religious views. Secular thinking can be as filled with prejudice, partiality and neglect of relevant data, and as intolerant of and impatient with opposition as the most narrow religious view. There is just no reasonable case for arguing that religious belief is as such irrational or unthinking. Any such view is plainly false. It is, in fact, a prime instance of irrational thinking.

Chapter 5
Life after death

Is belief in life after death harmful?

Having religious beliefs is not in itself dangerous, in the sense of being irrational. Nevertheless, some people hold that there is at least one sort of religious belief that does have harmful consequences. This is belief in an afterlife. One way in which this is said to be dangerous is that it may make people care less about what happens in this life, so that it does not matter much what you do to people. Also, you may not care too much whether you die, in battle or in a suicide bombing for example, which will make you much more dangerous to your enemies.

It is a constant theme of this book that over-generalisations about human beliefs are always misleading, and obscure the real issues at stake. It is vacuous to say that belief in life after death is always harmful. There are for a start many different sorts of belief about an afterlife. Suppose you believe that there exists a God of supreme compassion and love. If you let your life on earth be dominated by hatred, greed and the lust for power, you will naturally alienate yourself from such a God. Nevertheless, God will never cease to care for you. In the life after death, God will seek by all possible means to help you to turn away from hatred, and will always continue to draw you towards the divine love. In the end, given that God has infinite patience and time, it may well be that all conscious beings with a sense of personal continuity will be embraced fully by the divine love at last (will be 'saved' from hatred and its consequences).

Such a belief offers an ultimate hope of happiness and love

for all beings — that does not seem very harmful. Yet it does matter what people do during their earthly life. For they will have to undergo a time of training and discipline if they have done evil, aimed at the reformation of their characters. And justice requires that there should be rewards for good and punishments for evil. There will be punishment in a justly ordered universe. But such punishment will always leave open the possibility of reform and new life. It will never be solely vindictive or retributive.

If this is true, it will not matter too much if you die, for death is an entrance into greater life. But if you die while killing the innocent, this will entail punishment — a punishment that will continue until you have compensated in some way for the evil you have done, and have achieved some form of reformation.

This combination of just punishment, reformative discipline and ultimate redemption from evil is both just and compassionate. It is the belief of the majority of Jewish and Muslim theologians. There is a hell, a place of punishment. But it is not everlasting, and in Islam there is a reliable tradition from the Prophet that eventually all will be released from hell. In Hinduism and Buddhism, rebirth may be in one of a number of hells or heavens. But again eventually one can pay the price of one's own wrongdoing, and achieve final release from suffering. That possibility is never foreclosed for anyone, but our conduct on earth is vitally important in deciding whether we achieve it or not.

Traditional Christianity has perhaps had the harshest doctrine of hell, as a place of punishment from which there is no escape. But some notable theologians, including Origen, St Isaac the Syrian, St Gregory of Nyssa and Mother Julian of Norwich, have held the belief that all will eventually be saved. Pope John Paul II said that, while the church could not guarantee that all would be saved, it was certainly a possibility, and Catholics could rightly pray and hope for it. The Roman Catholic Church has long accepted purgatory as a place of purification for souls who will be saved, but who are not yet ready to stand in the presence of God. As Cardinal Bellarmine said, perhaps purgatory is full and hell is empty. On the most traditional view, souls only enter hell if they are irretrievably damned – that is, if they have turned against God in a completely final and irreversible way. And perhaps no one is in that situation.

As a Christian, I think it is very odd to believe that a God of love would send people to hell just for not having heard of Jesus, or for not having been baptised. At least, a God who did such things would not be a God of love in any sense of the word 'love' I can understand. Even so, this belief is not dangerous, since those who accept it (usually fundamentalist Protestants) also believe that it is their duty to preach the gospel to as many people as possible, and they think that no one can be forced into sincere belief. They hardly ever believe that violence could help to save people.

Most contemporary Christians probably think that hell is a state in which people find themselves in a world where greed, hatred and selfishness are unrestrained, and where they are the victims of the aggressive behaviour they displayed on earth. In such a world, they will be tormented by the flames of passion and locked into the 'outer darkness' of their own hearts. There will be bitterness instead of joy, frustration instead of fulfilment, and anger instead of calm. The world of hell is the world of unrestrained desire, where the destructive consequences of people's own egoistic behaviour are unleashed upon each other without the possibility of mitigation or escape.

The fear of hell, in other words, is the fear of a future without love and without God. Since the New Testament teaches that God wishes all to be saved – 'God our Saviour, who desires everyone to be saved' (1 Timothy 2:3-4) – Christians should be sure that God will do everything possible to bring sinners to repentance. But if human wills are free, there is a possibility that they may reject all advances of love, and remain locked into their own torment. How long will that last? It may be that a sense of duration is meaningless in hell. The twentieth-century Roman Catholic theologian Karl Rahner suggests that it could be 'eternal' in the sense of being beyond measured time – not torment going on for endless time, but just a state when one realises one's final exclusion from God.

For most Christians, those condemned to hell are those who finally, consciously and in full knowledge of the possibility of salvation, reject goodness and choose a life of malevolent desire. For traditional Christians, Jesus Christ is the only one who can liberate from the possibility of hell, the only 'name under heaven given among mortals by which we must be saved' (Acts 4:12). But Christ comes in many forms and guises. He is the 'true light which enlightens everyone' (John 1:9), and many Christians feel that people can be saved by one they may not have recognised on earth, but whom they will know as their saviour after death.

A future life of self-exclusion from joy and love is, for Christians and for many religious believers, a possibility for those whose lives are devoted to malevolent and egoistic desire. But the whole point of religion is to liberate people from that possibility, to draw them to a better life of joy and love. Thus if religion works properly, it is one of the major forces for happiness and goodness in the world. It is part of the teachings of most religions that 201 is so strong that it will corrupt religion, as it will corrupt everything else, where it can. Yet the primary intention of religion is deliverance from evil and devotion to goodness for its own sake. To call that dangerous requires an inversion of vision that is breathtaking.

Life after death as a motivation for morality

It would be wrong to terrify people with the thought that they might be tortured in hell for ever even for what seem quite trivial sins, like stealing or lying. I would think it is harmful to terrify people in that way. The Christian message is supposed to be one of forgiveness and divine love, and teaching about 'hell' – separation from God – should always be held together with teaching about God's unconditional forgiveness for all who trust in him, and God's limitless love for all human beings.

I certainly do not want to say that atheists are bound to be immoral, but I see no reason why atheists should care more about human life than theists do. Free from fear of hell, and having no hope of heaven, people are at liberty to act as they please, without consideration for consequences after death. If they want to kill, they can. If they want to end their own lives, why should they not? It just seems totally implausible to suggest that if you think there is an afterlife, you will be more likely to kill or commit suicide. If anything, people should be less likely to do so, because of what might happen to them after death. Of course, if some misguided individuals think they will be rewarded after death for killing innocent people, that is dangerous. But no mainstream religious tradition – not Judaism, not Islam, not Christianity – teaches such a thing. It is contrary to the central teaching of all major faiths, which is that compassion and mercy are obligatory for believers.

The reasons and the conditions under which one may kill a human being are matters for ethical debate. But considerations about life after death play no part in such debates. What is generally agreed is that if there is an afterlife there will be punishments for evil and rewards for good. That doctrine should bring fear only to those who are evil, and even for them it should offer hope for forgiveness.

As a matter of fact, belief in life after death is rarely a strong motivating factor in religion. Where it exists, it tends to be a consequence of other more important beliefs. Religion does not begin with belief in an afterlife, as though it began with wishful thinking and fear of death. Judaism, the best historically attested case of early religious belief, did not have a real belief in an afterlife at all until very late, towards the end of the period when the Hebrew Bible was written. There was a gloomy place called *Sheol* (in Latin, *Hades*), the world of the shades. But it was nothing to look forward to, just a dark sort of place where the remains of dead people gibbered and moaned and slowly mouldered away.

What Jews were interested in was not an afterlife, but having a good life now, and lots of children, and wine and food, and the worship and love of God, the God of the living. Judaism is a resolutely this-worldly religion, and even today you do not have to believe in an afterlife at all to be a good Jew.

Belief in resurrection developed around the time of the Maccabean revolt, in the second century BCE, when large numbers of Jews were being killed, and many began to be exercised by the problem of how a God of justice could let the lives of innocent and pious people be simply ended in such a way.

One source of belief in an afterlife is a prior belief that the universe is just – for this follows from belief in a just creator. Another similar source is belief that God wants people to have knowledge and love of the divine. Yet millions of people do not know God, and even those who do rarely love God with all their hearts and minds. Would a God with such a purpose not make it possible for human beings to know and love God properly? In which case, for the vast majority of people, that could only happen after death.

Belief in the resurrection of the body probably came from Persia, but it is a belief that the whole embodied person will exist again, in an environment where there is the possibility of communicating with others and of learning and developing in wisdom and understanding. But resurrection is not the resuscitation of these physical bodies. It is a different form of embodiment, not in this space and time at all, and its exact form cannot be imagined by us now. If there is a purgatorial, or intermediate, state of existence before the full vision of God, there may be one or more different forms of embodiment before we achieve that final embodiment that completes our existence. Or, as Gregory of Nyssa said, perhaps after death we continue on an endless journey into an infinite God, endlessly learning more of love and understanding.

In Indian religions, the same basic motivations – concern for cosmic justice and desire to know God or a supreme reality of wisdom, compassion and bliss more fully – led to an alternative supposition of rebirth. This does not have to be rebirth on earth, but involves the idea of continued existence in many different realms of being. It is thus not as different from belief in resurrection as some have supposed.

It is easy to dismiss such ideas as wishful thinking, especially if you are a materialist and you do not believe persons could survive the death of their bodies, since you will think they are no more than material bodies. But if you believe there is a spiritual basis to reality, and that the material cosmos is a means for bringing finite spirits into existence that can relate to one another in community, it will be impossible to think that people are just their bodies. Bodies will be seen as the vehicles of spirit, and we will naturally wish to enquire about the purpose of God in bringing such spirits into being and how that purpose can be realised.

Reflective thought will then lead us to think that each of our lives has a purpose, and to see that such a purpose cannot be realised for most human beings on earth. That will lead to the supposition of some form of life after death. Given experience of God and a revelation of God's nature and purpose (for Christians, the resurrection appearances of Jesus), our supposition will be confirmed. If the cosmos itself is rational and spiritual in nature, what we would rationally wish for could well, after all, be true.

So to the question of whether belief in life after death is dangerous or harmful, I would answer that certain sorts of belief – for example, that I will go to heaven only if I kill everyone who disagrees with me – would be harmful. People who believe that are either ignorant, criminal or insane. But belief in an afterlife as it is found in most major religions, far from being harmful, gives consolation to the bereaved, hope to the dying, motivation to the morally tempted and courage to those who are afraid. Such a belief may or may not be true. But it is certainly not dangerous. Karl Marx called it 'the heart of a heartless world'. A religious believer would say rather that the world at its deepest level is not heartless. It is human beings, lost in ignorance, hatred and greed, who are heartless. Religion exists to open a path to the healing of the human heart. It is precisely because human life on earth is felt to be of moral significance that the hope for life after death is a natural hope for the fulfilment of personal life in a reality that has been created by a personal God.

Part Three
Are religious beliefs immoral?

Chapter 6
Morality and the Bible

The problem of obsolete moral rules in the Old Testament

Religious morality is based on the belief that human life has moral significance, and that it is possible to overcome selfish egoism and attain a state or achieve a positive conscious relationship to a being of wisdom, compassion and bliss. This sounds the opposite of dangerous. But some people think that there is something dangerous about religious morality. That is because they think religious morality is based on unthinking acceptance of the rules of some holy book like the Bible. It might be bad enough to accept moral rules unthinkingly. But it is even worse if many of the moral rules in the Bible now seem to be cruel and reactionary. In the Old Testament, in particular, people can be stoned to death for adultery, for worshipping the wrong gods, even for disobedience to their parents. There do seem to be lots of what we would now call primitive moral ideas. Perhaps the worst of all can be found in Deuteronomy 20:16. It is called 'the Ban', and it reads: 'As for the towns of these peoples that the Lord your God is giving you as an inheritance, you must not let anything that breathes remain alive. You shall annihilate them – the Hittites and the Amorites, the Canaanites and the Perizzites, the Hivites and the Jebusites.' This applies only to Canaanite towns that make war against the Israelites, and do not submit peacefully. Even so, it is a pretty horrific scenario.

Reasons given for this command include the fact that no slaves or booty should be taken for personal use, and that the

Israelites should not assimilate to the customs of the Canaanite cities. But the fact remains that this is a savage attitude to war that few would accept today.

And that is the point. Moral attitudes have changed over the last three millennia, and sometimes they have changed for the better. If you leave God out of it altogether, and look at human attitudes to warfare, we can see developing over time a set of rules for limiting conduct in war. Such rules include a degree of protection for the innocent, regulations about the fair treatment of prisoners, and the prohibition of torture and needless cruelty.

As a matter of fact, the general rules for war in the Torah require that there should be no pre-emptive strikes, that women, children and animals should not be killed, and that fruit trees should not be destroyed. Later rabbinic commentary elaborated these rules to make it clear that loss of life should be minimised and that the environment should be safeguarded. However, the later history of Israel and its final ejection from its territories in 132 CE rendered most rules for warfare within Canaan obsolete. A central moral value for modern Jews is *shalom* – peace, wholeness and harmony. So for most Jews these rules for war are wholly obsolete, and cannot be used to undermine the prophetic obligation to work positively for peace and justice in society.

Modern rules for the conduct of war owe much to scholarly developments of biblical thought, and in particular to the Catholic 'just war' tradition, which developed principles governing Christian participation in war. In the thirteenth century Thomas Aquinas held that a justifiable war must be declared by a sovereign, must have a just cause (usually self-defence), and must have a realistic prospect of advancing good or avoiding evil. In the sixteenth century the legal theorist de Vitoria added that war must be waged by proper means, and that it must be discriminate (not, for instance, killing non-combatants) and proportionate (using minimal force to achieve a good end).

These rules are, like all moral principles, hotly debated, and it is not clear that they can be applied in conditions of modern warfare, where weapons of mass destruction have been used. But they illustrate the way in which religious institutions have devoted much thought to the question of the moral justification for killing, and have not simply quoted texts from the Bible. Indeed the whole tradition of Christian moral theology is based on rational reflection on the basic doctrines of creation and of rather general moral guidelines discerned in the life and often extremely cryptic teachings of Jesus. Biblical texts are usually quoted in support of particular arguments, but they are rarely decisive, and they are never the basis of moral debate.

Modern warfare is a terrible thing, and hardly anything more cruel or indiscriminately deadly than the saturation of cities with napalm gas or firebombs can be imagined. Cruelty and indiscriminate killing has not disappeared from the military practices of the most 'civilised' countries in the world.

Even so, the complete destruction of 'anything that breathes' is a pretty extreme practice. Such wholesale massacres do occur – they occurred in former Yugoslavia in the twentieth century, and they occurred in Soviet Russia, China and North Korea. But we hope that they are exceptions, to be condemned by the international community, not morally appropriate acts.

We hope that moral attitudes to war have developed in a more humane direction since the times when it was thought acceptable to slaughter whole city populations if they resisted military takeover. Such a humane development can undoubtedly be traced in the Bible. By the sixth century BCE, the prophet Ezekiel taught that each person should be punished only for their own sin – which rules out indiscriminate slaughter. And the Old Testament records many occasions when groups of Canaanites were not by any means destroyed. Hittites and Canaanites play an important part in the life of Israel: Tamar and Rahab, ancestors of Jesus, were Canaanites; Ruth, another ancestor, was a Moabitess; and Bathsheba, wife of King David, was married to Uriah the Hittite.

Most biblical scholars think that 'the Ban' was written long after the entry of the Israelites into Canaan, after the exile in Babylon, and that it was an imaginary version of the conquest of the land, extolling the irresistible power of the Israelites. It never actually happened like that, and such a rule was never put into practice, historically.

Even so, it is a bit of bloodthirsty imagination, and it could conceivably be taken to show that if God orders it, any moral monstrosity may become possible. It could, but no sane Jew would read it that way. The fact is that by the time the Ban was written down it was already obsolete. It never was an actual rule for the Jewish conduct of war, and it was already countermanded by other commands of the Torah, such as the famous 'an eye for an eye' command, which limits the amount of retribution to something proportionate to some committed offence – and, of course, that rule was in turn countermanded by later developments, for Christians most obviously by Jesus' teaching in the Sermon on the Mount.

So the Ban is a horrible rule, but most scholars believe it was never put into practice, and was obsolete even before it was written down. It would be slander to suggest that any Jew has ever seriously considered massacre to be ordered by God in any actual historical situation since the writing down of the Law.

A serious reading of the Bible makes it clear that moral perceptions of what God requires have developed in some respects over the centuries. In fact, saying that 'God requires X' is more or less equivalent to saying, 'I believe X is morally right.' It used to be thought, by many peoples, that it was morally right to massacre all one's enemies in battle. But as people reflected on what morality requires, they generally came to think that there should be some limits on the treatment of defeated enemies and their kin.

At least, it might be said, the Israelites were asking the question of what morality requires in war, and were not just saying that victors can do anything they feel like, or that moral issues are not at all relevant in war. They did not accept the concept of 'total war'. So the correct attitude to this biblical rule is, 'People used to think that it was right to massacre those who are defeated in battle, in certain circumstances (during the conquest of Canaan, when the Canaanites went to battle with the Israelites). But those circumstances cannot ever apply again, and consequently it will never again be right to massacre enemies.'

Three attitudes to ancient biblical texts

There are three basic religious attitudes that can be taken to this biblical rule and others like it in the Old Testament. The first is that they are examples of primitive moral attitudes, projected onto an imagined past, which were very rarely if ever put into practice, and are now totally obsolete. That is what an anthropologist might say, and in this respect the Bible parallels the sort of moral development that has taken place in most human societies. We might well say that the Bible shows a process of continuing moral reflection that is far in advance of most other human societies of the time. But nobody in their right mind would think of applying any of these ancient moral codes to society in the present day.

The second is that God really did give such a command, but only to people who were morally primitive and in the unique circumstance of the conquest of Canaan. The command is now obsolete, and must be seen in the context of a long subsequent history of rabbinic commentary and reflection. Such reflection has added many principles limiting the destructiveness and the conduct of war, and has emphasised the importance of having a goal of harmony and peace. This is what a conservative Christian might say, and it has the consequence that such rules do not give direct moral guidance now. It follows that even for the most conservative Christian, moral rules found in the Bible should not be taken out of context without bringing them into line with the more important rules of the Torah — such as 'love your neighbour as yourself' (Leviticus 19:18) — and without paying careful attention to the long tradition of rabbinic legal commentary and interpretation.

The third general religious attitude is that even the Ban expresses some perception of the divine will — in this case, a will for total devotion to God, and for the renunciation of all private gain from battle. But it was a very limited perception, which involved a distorted view of what God really requires (which is love of, or at least respect for, enemies). As such, it was corrected by developing perceptions of God's will by the later prophets of Israel.

This is the interpretation I prefer, and it entails that there is a developing understanding of God, a very useful record of which can be found in the Old Testament. At first God was taken to be a tribal war God (the God of Hosts, or armies), leading Israel to victory, and being one among many other gods — 'a great King above all gods' (Psalm 95:3). But by the time of the major prophets, in the eighth century BCE, God was seen to be the only true God, the creator of all things, whose will is for universal justice. It is the fully developed view that is important, not the primitive beginnings of the prophetic knowledge of God.

Whichever of these interpretations you take, nobody holds that commands such as that recorded in the Ban are to be applied at the present time. The main lesson is that you must read the particular rules of the Bible, especially of the Old Testament, in the light of later more developed moral views found within the Bible itself, which often render them obsolete or transform their interpretation.

Biblical language about God

The Hebrew Bible presents the story of how God's acts are intertwined with human hatred, greed and arrogant pride, and how God repeatedly raises up leaders and prophets to turn the people back towards a love of justice. That story, spanning millennia, contains many diverse perceptions of what God is doing and of how God acts. It is a story of developing perception of the will of God. It contains many primitive and imperfect perceptions, but these are counterbalanced and in the end transformed by the deeper perceptions of the great prophets.

The biblical viewpoint is that the world is corrupted by sin – by greed, hatred, arrogance and hypocrisy. The wars and massacres that litter human history are the results of a massive turning away from God and from devotion to goodness. The 'judgments of God' are the ways in which human egoism is self-destructive in the end. The wages of sin is death – the death of the soul, the death of goodness, the death of all true happiness and fulfilment.

It is possible to interpret the Bible very literally, and to suppose that the biblical God is an invisible person who punishes things he does not like by sending earthquakes and floods, and who gives long lists of fairly arbitrary commands that his worshippers are just to accept without question. But such a literal reading is untrue to the long tradition of Jewish and Christian theological reflection. Jewish and Christian theologians are agreed that the Bible speaks in vivid metaphors about God that are not to be taken as literal descriptions. When God is said to enjoy the smell of a good sacrifice, we are not supposed to think that God has nostrils, and literally likes breathing in the smell of roasting meat. God has no body and no bodily sense-organs. What is expressed in such pictures is that God is pleased when humans show their commitment to reverence of supreme goodness and beauty (when they do so sincerely) by offering something of value to God – which symbolises the offering of their own lives to the service of goodness.

Even then, we are not to think of God as being cheered up when he is depressed, or of God being pleased when humans grovel and utter all sorts of obsequious and flattering sentiments. We have to get rid of all anthropomorphism, and recognise that metaphorical talk about God is a way of saying what humans should do and how they should see their lives in the context of a supreme reality of ultimate goodness. When we say that 'God is pleased', we are expressing the fact that we fulfil the purpose of our lives when we orient them to supreme goodness and seek to let such goodness be expressed through us.

This is not some modern, trendy reworking of the idea of God. It is written into the texts themselves, and is the unanimous teaching of major theologians such as Augustine and Aquinas (in Christianity), Maimonides (in Judaism) and Al Gazzali (in Islam). Thus Aquinas said that there is never any change in God at all. God is changeless in perfection. When we speak of God being pleased or angry, we are really speaking about changes in human life and attitudes, changes perhaps in how we see God, but not in how God is.

The prohibition of making any 'carved images' of God is an expression of this teaching that nothing in all finite creation is like God. For the Jewish tradition, God cannot be adequately represented by any finite form, and so in the Holiest Place in the Temple there was no statue of God. God remains the Unknowable, beyond human understanding. God is certainly not a person who has tantrums like a human tyrant. For God is one 'with whom there is no variation or shadow due to change' (James 1:17).

So in the Bible the idea of God develops as a way of affirming that the world has a fundamental moral order. The 'wrath of God' is a way of talking about the self-destructiveness of evil. The 'love of God' is a way of talking about the fulfilment of human life in positive relationship to a Supreme Good. That Supreme Good exists, and it is the foundation of the whole cosmos. But we can speak of it only by speaking of how human beings relate to it, indirectly and by means of metaphor.

Part of the message of the book of Job is that we must not think of God too anthropomorphically, as a person who distributes rewards and punishments in accordance with human virtue and vice. And it is more characteristic of Jewish biblical meditation continually to question God than to blindly accept whatever God says. Very often, the beginning of wisdom in religion is to learn to distinguish between literal description and metaphor, and then to learn that metaphors in religion have the function of guiding human feelings and behaviour, aspirations and hopes.

Jewish attitudes to biblical laws

An orthodox Jew will certainly accept that God gave the Law to Moses. But how that Law is to be interpreted and applied is very much a matter for discussion. For Jews, the Torah is not a list of rules that anyone can read and apply literally in modern life. The Torah needs to be interpreted by rabbinic reflection and debate. So, by the time the Talmud was written down (in the third century CE) all the laws concerning polygamy, stoning to death and the conduct of war had long been rendered obsolete. Religious law, like any body of laws, develops and is interpreted by lawyers or religious scholars. The specific laws of the Old Testament and the Talmud are like precedents that can be amended, amplified or reinterpreted as new occasions arise. In Judaism, the Law is a living tradition, and professional lawyers, the rabbis, have the job of applying old rules to new cases – or of deciding that the old rules do not apply any more. Orthodox Jews have no difficulty in saying that there are rules in the Old Testament that we would now regard as morally primitive. But, they might well say, the fact we now see them as morally primitive is largely due to the prophetic tradition of seeking to discern the divine will more fully in the light of experience and a deeper understanding of what God requires.

Jews can cheerfully say that there are many obsolete and primitive moral rules in the Hebrew Bible. This is because the Hebrew Bible is a very good record of the developing moral perceptions of the Jewish people. This record parallels that of most ancient cultures, but there is little doubt that the idea of one creator God concerned for justice and for the flourishing of creation originated with the prophets of ancient Judaism. There is a crucial emphasis on justice and mercy, on concern for widows, the old, the poor, resident foreigners and the oppressed, and on the duties of open-handed giving and taking responsibility for the disadvantaged. The land is to be cultivated responsibly, and not despoiled. All debts are to be released, property returned to its original owners, and slaves freed, every fifty years. By the time of Jesus, rabbinic interpreters of the Law regarded many of the older rules – for instance, concerning the right of private retribution and polygamy – as obsolete, and offered various interpretations of the remaining food laws, laws of religious ritual, and laws enjoining charity and care for dependants and the poor. After the destruction of the Temple in 70 CE, most of the ritual laws and laws referring to the 'promised land' also became obsolete. So the Torah is now partly a set of rules, such as food and Sabbath laws, that set Jews apart as a people called to witness to the sovereignty of God, and partly a set of moral exhortations to social responsibility, kindness, justice and mercy. It is only when the religious Law is seen as a holistic set of living, changing, dynamic principles underlying the life of a specific community that specific biblical rules can be placed in their proper historical context.

It would be quite wrong to think that Jews then or Jews now would simply point to rules in the Hebrew Bible and say, 'We must do this.' Such an attitude would be regarded by them as unprofessional and ignorant. What has to take place is long and detailed discussion of how the underlying principles of the Torah are to be applied. Knowledge of a variety of different historical interpretations, and knowledge of previous rabbinical precedents, is always a part of this process. To fail to see this is simply to fail to see what living Judaism is.

The Sermon on the Mount

Christian thinking on biblical morality is deeply affected by the fact that Christians have given up the Torah, as a complete system of God-given rules all of which they have to obey. In the first Christian generation, largely because of the large number of Gentile converts to the new faith, Christians abandoned the food laws and the laws of religious observance and ritual purity that had existed to set Jews apart as a covenant people. They also set aside specific laws about slavery and property and family (which allowed limited slavery and polygamy), thus regarding the vast majority of Old Testament rules as obsolete.

As the apostle Paul said, 'Christ is the end of the Law' (Romans 10:4), and he wrote that the whole Law is summed up in loving your neighbour as yourself (Galatians 5:14). The moral ideal, for Christians, is to be found not in a written text ('the letter kills, but the Spirit gives life', wrote Paul in 2 Corinthians 3:6), but in the dynamic person of Jesus, who is the living and personal Word of God. So it is to the teachings and the life of Jesus that Christians look to find their moral inspiration.

Christianity is not a religion of a written law, but a religion of grace, of God's love given unconditionally in a human person, the person of Jesus. So for Christians, morality finds its culmination in the life and teaching of Jesus, and there can be no question that every moral rule in the Bible is transformed when it is seen in the light of the self-giving love of Jesus.

Jesus had a very humane attitude to religious and moral laws. He strongly criticised the legalism of some Pharisees, who seemed to be more concerned with rigorous adherence to rules than with care for human well-being. When he healed on the Sabbath, when his disciples ate corn on the Sabbath, when he touched lepers and corpses, and when he ignored traditional rules of washing and fasting, he pointed out that the 'weightier matters of the law', loving-kindness and care for others, were more important than observance of minor regulations that were in any case capable of various interpretations.

Matthew records the main teaching of Jesus about morality in the so-called Sermon on the Mount (Matthew chapters 5–7). In that teaching, Jesus denies that he is abandoning the Torah, but he does take it upon himself to reinterpret it in quite a radical way. So in the five 'Great Antitheses' (Matthew 5:21–48), Jesus says, 'You have heard... but I say to you...' It is not just killing that is wrong, but anger. It is not just adultery that is wrong, but seeing others solely as objects of sexual desire. It is not just breaking an oath that is wrong, but all untruth. You should not just confine justice to exacting a fair penalty, you should be ready to forgive evil. You should not love your neighbour and hate your enemy, you should love your enemy also.

In this series of astonishing statements – so astonishing that it seems highly probable that they must go back to an outstanding moral teacher, and there is good reason to think this was Jesus himself – the religious Law is not abandoned. But it is interpreted in such a way that most of its specific commands are rendered obsolete. The Law, Jesus teaches, is not to be simply cast aside as worthless. But it is to be fulfilled and transcended by a more inward, more universal and more demanding morality. Not just outer acts of killing, adultery and oath-breaking, but inner attitudes of anger, lust and untruthfulness, are condemned. Concern to limit punishment is extended to throw doubt on the appropriateness of any purely retributive punishment. And the limitation of love to neighbours is extended to all people without exception, including enemies.

The fulfilment of the Law is seen to be unrestricted love and concern for the welfare of others. And such concern is to be a matter of the heart, not just of external observance. It is not surprising that when Jesus was asked what the most important laws were, he picked out two (neither of them, incidentally, in the Ten Commandments) – the love of God and love of your neighbour as yourself (Matthew 22:36–40). Those are the laws by which all others are to be interpreted or, where needed, rendered obsolete.

If Christians take the Sermon on the Mount seriously, they have to see the Torah as pointing towards, and being fulfilled in, the teaching that universal unrestricted love is the key moral principle. Luke's parables of the Good Samaritan and the Prodigal Son illustrate this point vividly by stressing that vindictiveness and resentment have no place in love, and that no one is excluded from the universality of love.

In view of the clear teaching of Jesus, it is a gross misunderstanding of Christian morality to say that Christians have to obey a lot of primitive moral rules just because they are to be found in the pages of the Bible. For Christians, the key ethical teaching is to be found in Jesus' Sermon on the Mount, and all other moral rules in the Bible have to be judged by how far they meet the standards of that sermon.

Was Jesus morally perfect?

Most Christians would agree that the standards of the Sermon on the Mount are illustrated in the life of Jesus himself, who shows the divine love as fully as it can be shown in human form. Nevertheless, there are those who find the life of Jesus himself less than morally perfect. Writers such as the philosopher Bertrand Russell (in his short essay, *Why I am Not a Christian*) accuse Jesus of moral imperfection by pointing to the cleansing of the Temple, which seems to have been an intolerant and violent act. They point out that Jesus called the Pharisees and lawyers 'whited sepulchres', hypocrites and blind guides, which seems rather uncharitable. He spoke a lot about the flames of hell and the danger of judgment, which seems very judgmental. And he cursed a poor fig tree, which had done nothing wrong, but just failed to produce figs – out of season, too. Was he really such a saint, after all?

Was Jesus a violent, intolerant, judgmental and petulant character? All we know about Jesus comes from the four Gospels, and they certainly intended to represent Jesus as 'without sin', so it would be very surprising if they had unintentionally portrayed him as quite an unpleasant character. He healed, he forgave sins, he mixed with socially borderline people, in parables and stories he taught the necessity of unlimited self-giving love, he claimed to bring people into a closer relationship with God, and he accepted a violent death rather than betray his commitment to God. That is quite a good start.

But was he violent? He did not foment revolution against the military occupying power of the Roman empire or against Herod the puppet-king. He taught that you should turn the other cheek, and that the meek were blessed. He resisted the attempts of the common people to proclaim him king. So how could anyone think he was violent? Well, he took a whip, says John's Gospel, and drove the money changers from the Temple precincts. He drove out cattle and overturned tables. It does not say, however, that anyone was hurt. This was certainly decisive action against commercial activities in God's Temple. Are we to suppose that it is always wrong to use moderate force to eject undesirables from our property? This account shows that Jesus was not always 'meek and mild', passively putting up with anything. He could take decisive action to remedy what he saw as sacrilege in his Father's house. I cannot see anything unacceptably violent about that. It seems to me to show courage and resolution, without actually physically harming anyone.

Was he intolerant? He did criticise the lawyers and Pharisees in strong language. But again, may they not have deserved it? It is noteworthy that Jesus did not insult the poor or the marginalised. He insulted the privileged, the religious leaders, those who claimed to possess the authority of God, but who were actually arrogant and self-satisfied. If what they were doing was wrong and deceitful, was it not appropriate to criticise them? It is a very strange notion of moral goodness that does not allow you to criticise hypocrites and deceivers who pervert religion and morality. Again, no violence was used, and there was no danger of anyone being ostracised or harmed by Jesus' attacks. He was a social outsider, mocking the rich and powerful and exposing their deceits. I think that was morally justifiable – and probably good fun, too, for those poor people who heard him.

All right, then, what about hell and judgment? The simple answer is that if there is hell and judgment, then we could hardly expect Jesus not to mention the fact. He undoubtedly called for repentance, and offered eternal life to all who turned to God, so he was not telling people that they were going to hell whether they liked it or not. He was telling people that they need not go to hell, and offering them a free pardon. He made it quite clear that he made this offer to all, and especially to those who were sinners and not morally upstanding citizens. That is hardly being judgmental. It is just about as merciful as you can get.

It may be held that belief in hell is in itself harmful. I have dealt with that question in the previous chapter. If there is divine judgment, the fact will have to be mentioned, whether it is harmful or not. It should be remembered that the whole point of the Christian gospel is to avoid hell and to forgive guilt. It is not to tell people that they are going to hell. It is to tell them how to avoid hell. It is to warn them of the seriousness of judgment on their actions, and to promise that

God in Christ has taken that judgment on himself. Some people may find that odd, but it is hardly harmful.

Finally, what about the fig tree? Nobody was harmed in this episode. If it happened, it was most likely an acted parable, to warn the disciples that if their lives were not fruitful, they would be in danger of destruction, or to warn Israel of destruction if it failed to reform its ways. The story may have been a literalisation of an actual parable (found in Luke), which had been transformed in the telling. Either way, it does not show that Jesus was cruel to any conscious being.

My conclusion is that there are no serious objections to the moral perfection of Jesus. And, most importantly, the main lesson is that we should interpret the life of Jesus in the light of the whole Bible, and of the main events and teachings in it – the Sermon on the Mount, the parables of forgiveness, love and eternal life, and Jesus' death on the cross. Jesus was a man of healing power, forgiving love, identification with the outcast – and also, these points show, of courage in seeking purity of faith, relentless criticism of the arrogant and hypocritical in religion, and a deep concern for the ultimate welfare of all people.

This does seem to me to be a standard of what a human life should be. But above all, Jesus' life was a life of prayer, of constant and undivided attention to his heavenly Father, and of dedication to his Father's will. It is in that deep centredness in prayer that the secret of moral life is to be found. It is from that resource that the divine love can flood into a world of suffering and hatred. It is there that the joy of eternity can assuage the hurts and inevitable frustrations of time.

Religious law and its interpretation

Christian moral standards should be quite clear. They are based on understanding of the life and teaching of Jesus, and have replaced a set of religious laws with the Gospel records of the person of Jesus.

Christianity is not a religion of revealed divine law at all, and so it is particularly inappropriate to think that it is possible to solve moral problems just by quoting ancient biblical laws. Of course it is possible to find people who do precisely that. In April 2006 the members of the Westboro Baptist Church, Topeka, Kansas, demonstrated at the funerals of American soldiers killed in Iraq with placards reading, 'Thank God for Dead Soldiers' and 'God Hates Fags'. Their pastor justifed the action by saying that soldiers who defended a 'fag nation' (in other words, America) deserved no respect.

This sounds rather worrying. But it turns out that the church in question consists of seventy-six members of the pastor's extended family. The only appropriate comment one can make is that irrational prejudice does exist, and that nobody can stop an unbalanced individual from starting his own church, stocking it with his own family, and using it to publicise his own shockingly corrupt views. Perhaps he is even now organising a world tour to find any remaining Amalekites and stone them to death, as the Old Testament recommends. With luck, he may be away for a very long time.

The attitudes of the vast majority of Christians are very different from this, and to take such weird cases as typical of religion is like taking the British National Party to be representative of the Conservative Party. Of course there are religious people who are prejudiced, ignorant, repressed, obsessive, neurotic, unbalanced or completely mad. But to form a dispassionate assessment of religion requires that we pay more attention to the sane, intelligent and morally committed members of major religious communities. If we do that, we shall find that the history of Christian moral thought does not consist in quoting biblical texts out of context. It appeals to the person and teaching of Christ as the criterion by which to judge all biblical teachings. This is not a matter of obeying written rules without question. It calls for sensitive judgment, for a balanced interpretation of the person of Jesus, and for a good deal of personal decision-making in applying basic moral principles to particular situations. In other words, Christian moral reasoning is precisely that — reasoned argument about what is best for loving one's neighbour as oneself, in the light of the life of Jesus, who is the supreme exemplar of self-giving love.

This is true of Christianity. But religions of law, of the Torah and *Shari'a*, also require reasoned argument to interpret the law in new situations. The commands and prohibitions of the law are very rarely taken literally, and various traditions of interpretation exist, allowing a great deal of room for creative moral decision-making. There is bound to be disagreement about moral decisions, but we should at least recognise that decisions are being made, arguments deployed and reasons given.

It is not the case, in any instructed religious community, that ancient commands are just being blindly and unquestioningly obeyed. Most religious moralities do not depend on blind obedience to some ancient written text. Much more important are the interpretations and applications of moral principles that are sometimes only implicit in the scriptures, and that often need to be formulated in new ways in new situations. Critics may still disagree with some of the conclusions of religious ethicists. But at least they should realise that they are disagreeing with complex processes of moral reasoning, informed both by scripture and by a continually developing understanding of human nature and the natural world.

Even though there are religious sects that may apply the rules of archaic texts literally to modern conditions, such sects are not representative of the great world religious traditions. In the case of those great traditions, their methods of moral reasoning are so widely recognised that religious leaders are routinely consulted on moral matters by many major governmental agencies throughout the world. Far from being considered dangerous, religious morality is widely considered to be a valuable resource for moral thinking in the modern world. That judgment is more likely to be correct than the diatribes of those who travesty and lampoon what religious moral thinking is really like.

Chapter 7
Morality and faith

A non-religious account of morality

Religious morality may not be dangerous. But many people might argue that religion is, or should be, irrelevant to morality. They argue that morality does not depend upon religion, and indeed that it is somehow irrational or immoral to try to make it do so. That is not so clear to me, and I will indulge in a little autobiography to try to explain why I have come to think that a morality that does depend upon some form of religious belief is more reasonable than one that does not. I am not arguing that you have to be religious to be moral, or that religious people are more moral than non-religious people. I am arguing that there is an important connection between religious and moral belief. Some forms of religious belief provide stronger justifications for some forms of moral belief than can any non-religious view. Whether or not you think that is a good thing may depend on your own moral beliefs, or lack of them.

I began my university teaching career in 1964, as a lecturer in philosophy at the University of Glasgow. Many (not by any means all) of the best philosophers in Britain in those days were atheists, and I was very much influenced by them. I rejoiced that I did not have to bow to the will of some tyrannical sky-god. I was free to enjoy the wonder and luck of life without worrying about hell or repressing my desires in the vain hope of some future heaven. I could make my own moral decisions, and morality would be based on empathy or natural compassion or on the reasonable requirements of living together in security.

The trouble was that, as a professional philosopher, I preferred ideas to messy personal relationships. I could see every reason to pursue my desires at the expense of others if I could get away with it. And I had very little compassion; indeed, I probably cared more about stray cats in my neighbourhood than I did about unseen human beings starving to death in faraway places. To me, morality was an accidental by-product of successful evolutionary strategies in the far past, which my own hard-headed reason might be able to overcome and set aside in the present.

Why should I care about what helped my remote ancestors to breed successfully? Do I really care about the propagation of my genes? I might not be able to do anything about it if my beliefs really are genetically programmed into me. But what if I have a certain amount of rational control over my beliefs, if I can actually consider evidence, follow arguments and change some of my beliefs by thinking hard and carefully? In that case I am free to decide that I do not care about propagating my genes, and that I will evade the genetic programmes causing me to behave in specific (sometimes altruistic) ways, wherever they are inconvenient. The crunch question is: what will I put in their place? It seems to me that the only reasonable basis of action is to satisfy the desires that I have. It takes a lot of reasoning to discover what my desires really are, what desires I have a hope of satisfying, and how to order those desires in the best way.

My desires will not all be selfish, by any means. I might love my wife and desire her happiness. I might love my children, or my country, or even (improbably) the human race. On the whole, evolutionary psychologists seem to be right that most of the desires we have express loyalty to our kinship groups and sexual partners. This probably is due to our long evolutionary history – desires probably are genetically based, to a large degree, so our present desires do tell us what were good evolutionary strategies in the distant past.

Where reason comes in is in the identification of our
desires, their ranking in order of importance and feasibility,
and our assessment of the best way of realising them. This
involves self-knowledge, prudence and practical wisdom. And
it does allow for the construction of a rational morality. For I
will depend on other people for many of the things I need to
flourish, and I will need to work out principles of action that
will enable us to trust and work with one another with a fair
degree of reliability. Moral rules, basically, will be the rules we
agree to accept that enable us to make plans in common with
others, and that establish a degree of predictability in human
affairs.

Moral rules are conventions that cause us to restrict or
modify our desires — to accept compromises in the different
desires that different people seek to satisfy — in order to live
predictably with others. But they are vitally important
conventions, which need to be reinforced by sanctions, for
without them social life would be chaotic.

Evolutionary psychology can help us to see why we have the
basic desires that we do have (they are genetically programmed
from past evolutionarily stable strategies). It can also help us
not to be too unrealistic about what can be expected of human
beings (they are capable of limited altruism, but are basically
aggressive and promiscuous also — at least the males are).

Reason and desire

But evolutionary psychology sometimes tends to go further
and hypothesise that the human sense of moral obligation, or
conscience, is itself nothing more than a genetically
programmed compulsion or belief. When I feel 'I morally
ought to do this', that feeling of 'ought'-ness is a belief and an
associated feeling caused by my genes, which were selected
because they produced survival-enhancing behaviour a million
years ago. It follows that if I can now escape the tyranny of

genetic programming, it is rational to do so. I must examine all the feelings of obligation I have, to see whether they can be rationally justified – and that means seeing whether they conduce to the realisation of my desires, given the limitations imposed by my own prudential selected desire-realisation programme and by the compromises expected of me by my society.

This is indeed a sensible policy. If I feel an obligation not to step on the cracks of a pavement, I can see that this obligation has no rational justification in terms of any good such a policy may achieve. But there are some problems. Just by using my reason, I can see that my pleasure is not, in the universal scheme of things, more important than the pleasure of anyone else. Reason enjoins impartiality. If my desire for pleasure justifies my seeking pleasure, then everyone's desire for pleasure justifies their seeking pleasure. So I have to admit that it is rational for everyone to seek pleasure; as rational as it is for me to do so.

If 'good' is the object of rational desire, then pleasure is a good for every sentient being. Now comes the move on which John Stuart Mill's famously invalid argument for utilitarianism depends. But I will put it in a form that is not invalid. If pleasure is a good for everyone, then *if I aim at the good*, I will aim at the pleasure of all, not just of myself. The move here is from an actual desire that I have (my own pleasure) to a rational policy for which I may have no desire at all (to seek the good of all). An impartial observer – say, for instance, God – would no doubt seek the pleasure of all, for God has no partial desires. But if it is reasonable for me to pursue my desires, and for everyone else to pursue their desires, and if everyone desires pleasure, it does not at all follow that it is reasonable for anyone to pursue the pleasure of everyone (that is the invalid move made by Mill). For they may very well have no desire to do so.

Still I may see that the pleasure of everyone is a good thing, and a better thing than the pleasure of only a few people.

Reason can frame the concept of something that is good, something that is an object of rational desire, even if no one desires it (they would desire it if they were purely or impartially rational). Reason can look impartially at the universe and see that the more rational desires that are satisfied, the better things are. But now reason is beginning to get the better of desire. Now it is possible to say, 'It is a good thing to have a desire for universal happiness,' even when no one actually has such a desire. This is something human beings *ought* to desire. The 'moral ought' has crept in, and it is neither a genetic survival of past fecundity, nor an actual desire that anyone may have. It is this moral ought – not necessarily, and perhaps rarely, an actual desire, and yet perfectly rational – that is the problem for evolutionary psychology, and for all accounts of morality that are based solely on desire.

Evolutionary psychologists may say that we should not expect people to have such implausibly universal desires. It is enough to work with the desires we have, and to expect no more than limited altruism and whatever desires are necessary to make modern society work smoothly.

Even this modest proposal gives reason an important role in shaping desires. Human desires are extremely varied, and people do not always have the rather moderate and conformist desires of the lower middle classes. There are people who want plastic surgery to be turned into cats. There are people who want to possess slaves and subject whole populations to tyranny. There are people who want to rape, murder and pillage. And there are people who want to break the moral rules to their own advantage. And all these people can, in the right circumstances, get away with it.

It will accomplish very little to take them to one side and say, 'Let's be reasonable. You must moderate your desires and compromise a little.' The likely result is that you will get shot. In actual human societies, morality is, as Nietzsche pointed out, the rules of the herd, 'only for little people', as one famous American capitalist said. So, while we can find good reasons why people should have prudent and moderate desires, and enter into compromises and contracts with others, those reasons will only really count with those who are suggestible enough, or who stand to gain enough, to acknowledge their utility. And even then, given the opportunity, there is not an overwhelming reason to keep the rules at all times and in all situations, whatever the consequences.

That is what the well-known English philosopher Philippa Foot meant when she said that morality was in a sense 'a confidence trick', and what the Darwinian philosopher Michael Ruse meant when he called morality a trick played on us by our genes.

Can goodness exist objectively?

Fortunately, human beings are rarely completely consistent. Despite this depressing outcome of a morality founded solely on actual human desires, a great many people feel quite passionately that social justice, truth and genuine (non-kin-based) altruism are moral values that should be pursued even at great personal cost. Morality has a firmer base than desire alone can logically provide. It is based, at least for many people, on an implicit belief in the objectivity and 'commandingness' of the ideals of truth, beauty and goodness. It is to such ideals that human desires should be directed. That is what impartial reason teaches, and if it is asked why impartial reason should have any sway with us, one powerful answer is to point to a basic rational order and to the objective existence of goodness in the cosmos.

Even the French philosopher Jean-Paul Sartre, who wrote that 'moral seriousness' – belief in the objectivity of goodness – is actually a form of inauthentic human life, changed his mind when confronted with starving children in Algeria. In the course of an interview on French television, he stated that he came to see that he was not free to reject the obligation to help. Morality was, after all, objective in some sense. Sartre at that point became a Marxist rather than an existentialist.

I never became a Marxist. But I realised that I, too, did not really believe I was free to decide that whatever I liked was good – to let people starve to death if I felt like it. Perhaps an objective standard of goodness actually did exist. Perhaps I really did believe in truth, honesty and sincerity after all. But how could I justify such a belief?

I did not doubt that morality can exist without faith; fortunately, most humans do have a natural moral sense. But when intelligent humans begin to question the very basis of morality – what goodness truly is and why we should pursue it – it becomes vitally important to clarify our view of human nature, the value of our pursuits and our place in reality. As I reflected on these things – it was, after all, my job to do so as a philosopher – I began to pay more attention to the great classical tradition of philosophy, with its roots in Plato and its close historical connection with Christianity. Perhaps, as so many great philosophers had held, the fundamental nature of reality is spiritual and not material. Perhaps truth, beauty and goodness are inherent in the nature of things, based in a spiritual reality, a reality of supreme truth, beauty and goodness, from which the whole material cosmos issues. Perhaps the basic religious claim is true, that there exists a supreme goodness that is the basis of all reality, and which is the object of our deepest desires and hopes.

Avoiding literalism

First, however, choices had to be made. I certainly would not defend every doctrine that religious believers had uttered. Some religious views – for instance, the view that God issues a set of commands that are to be obeyed, even against the promptings of conscience; or that morality is irrelevant to faith, since we are saved by grace; or that most people are condemned to eternal hell, whatever they do — seemed to me morally abhorrent. But the religious belief that there exists an objective and supreme Good, that there is a power that can help people to be good (or at least better), and that goodness will at last triumph over evil in the world, meaning that human moral efforts are never in vain, offered a distinct basis for moral action. Christianity, I started to see, is not about tyrannical sky-gods, but about the objectivity of goodness.

As I argued in the previous chapter, morality cannot be founded on a simple appeal to biblical authority alone, any more than the basic rules of life can come from human nature and desires alone, which are often egoistic. When we look closely at the Gospels, we see that Jesus prepared people from the start to question accepted rules when they seemed harmful to human dignity and flourishing. Jesus never advocated taking a life and taught that even enemies should be loved. He taught that those who would be leaders should be the servants of all and that his followers should never respond to violence with violence. When Jesus was asked what the basic moral rules were for his disciples, he cited just two — love of God and love of neighbour. Healing, forgiveness, and reconciliation, he stressed in his teaching on the Torah, were more important than keeping rules for their own sake.

Jews and Muslims have their own models to follow, which I honour and respect. But for me Jesus is the one who disclosed what God is really like. And central to the Christian view of morality is the idea that traditional rules should be questioned, laws may be abrogated by later insights, and the deeper principles that underlie moral rules can be mined from the texts and applied in new ways. Christian morality is based on the teaching of Jesus, yes, but that very teaching questions all traditional rules to see whether they lead to human fulfilment, flourishing, and loving one's neighbour as oneself. At times, the best interpretation of a law may require a renunciation of its literal sense. For example, Jesus' teaching makes rules like 'Stone adulterers to death' or 'an eye for an eye' completely inapplicable, without actually saying they are wrong.

If we move from blind obedience to instructed discernment, we can be more ready to radically reinterpret specific moral rules of the Bible, as Jesus did, if, when applied literally, they contradict the basic moral principle of loving our neighbours as ourselves. We can amend these kinds of rules in light of the gospel's call for equal respect of all humans.

Religious morality has always been a matter of reflection and argument, and the most important texts of all the major religions bring to the foreground the criterion by which our morals should be assessed: do the rules lead us to treat others the way we would treat ourselves, or not? The Christian view certainly is that you cannot love God if you do not love your neighbour, and you should love your neighbour because every human person has a unique importance and dignity.

Religion and true humanism

Since the twentieth century, the threat of the destruction of the earth has focused attention on the millions who are poor and starving in the developing world. Advances in molecular biology, evolutionary theory and ecology have illuminated the interconnectedness of the natural world and have prompted in many people a greater concern for all living things. Interest in the flourishing of all beings has been placed on the moral agenda of most religious traditions, and it is religion that can help lead us all to a true human moral community. To the humanist dimension, religion adds a rationale for commitment to human freedom and dignity, a firm faith that moral action is never useless, and the fact that goodness objectively exists. For believers, morality is personal and inward, part of a life-transforming relationship of responsible and enduring love with the creator of the world rather than a matter of social convention.

God is not some sort of arbitrary tyrant, promulgating absurd rules that humans must just accept. God is apprehended as one who has a purpose in creation, and who gives human beings a part to play in realising that purpose. The purpose of God is, broadly speaking, that societies of finite personal beings should come to exist, who can grow in knowledge and understanding, in synergy (cooperation) and empathy (compassion) with one another, and in the creation and appreciation of the beauty and intricate structure of the world. This is a growth towards greater conscious appreciation of love, beauty and truth. Such growth is a moral duty, an absolute obligation, because it is what God wills, and it is built into the structure of human life, so that humans only find true happiness in the pursuit of goodness.

Such a religiously based morality could be called a sort of transcendental humanism, for what it aims at is the fulfilment and flourishing of all human goods. It is not at all world-denying or negative about human life. It is transcendental because the ideals of human life are rooted in the transcendent personal reality of God. In the end, they are fulfilled in the vision of God, in the clear knowledge of the divine presence, power, wisdom and beauty – the 'glory' – of God.

This means that morality has a specific character and tone. It is not laborious obedience to a set of impersonal moral rules. It is a living relationship to a personal God of supreme goodness. The believer does what is right because the believer has been grasped by a vision of supreme personal goodness, by a glimpse of the vision of God. Thereafter, all life is a quest for a clearer, fuller vision of goodness. God is obeyed because God is loved, and because doing the will of the Beloved is the greatest pleasure life offers. It is because the pursuit of the vision of God becomes life's greatest purpose that the believer will do those things that are conducive to realising that purpose – and those things are called 'duties'. They are not just rules that we have made up. They tell us what we must do if we are to know and love God more fully and truly.

Between seeing morality as a necessary basic framework for social stability and seeing morality as the path to union with God there is a world of difference. But both of these are different from seeing morality as obedience to the rigid rules of a primitively imagined sky-god. There is no such god, frightening us into obeying arbitrary rules out of fear of torture in hell; that is the god of sick minds and corrupted wills.

But what did a purely atheistic creed offer? Well, one could still believe in the importance of truth, beauty and friendship. Yet these seem to be purely personal preferences or hard-wired evolutionary survivals that one might disable, if they could be manipulated to personal advantage. While I felt distaste for that possibility, I could not justify my feeling. Why on earth was truth important? I could not escape the paradox that truth is only important if I decide it is, and if it is just a personal option I should feel no compunction in discarding it if I feel like it. So I started to look again more closely at the religious option, and to the possibility of faith – primarily, faith in an objectively existing goodness, beauty and truth; in a word, in God.

My case for founding morality on religion is simply that, at the deepest level, the firmest rational foundation for morality seems to me to be the objective existence of a supreme being who defines what goodness is – a being of wisdom, creativity, sensitivity and bliss. To that understanding, faith adds an insistent moral demand, a responsibility to care for the world that God has created.

Believers have no magical route to moral certainty, nothing that undercuts the hard process of moral analysis and reflection. Like everyone else, believers have to get involved in arguments as to what love requires in a very ambiguous world. There can be religious beliefs that are infantile, ugly and pathological. There can be moral codes that are intolerant, repressive and divisive. In comparing secular and religious morality, we need to compare the worst with the worst, and the best with the best. That means comparing the atrocities of Josef Stalin or Adolf Hitler with the atrocities of the Aztecs or the witch-burners. And it means comparing the humanism of John Stuart Mill with the ideals of St Francis.

Both the latter are to be admired. But in my view, secular humanism is built on shifting soil, as there is no objective moral demand, no objective remedy for human weakness, no objective hope for the final realisation of virtue and happiness. I have no wish to condemn secular humanist morality, but for me, it lacks the depth and vision and power of a morality based on belief in the objectivity of beauty and goodness, and on the possibility of human lives being brought to fulfilment by sharing in the divine will. Perhaps, as Erasmus saw, humanism – belief in the dignity and unique value of personal life – cannot really survive without some form of faith in a supremely personal God who gives to humanity its dignity and hope.

Chapter 8
The Enlightenment, liberal thought and religion

Was the Enlightenment the age of reason?

Belief in God and in life after death do not seem to be any more harmful than atheism or the belief that this is the only life there is. Both sets of beliefs can be felt to be liberating and to make human life on earth of great importance, or they can give rise to moral indifference. Nevertheless, some people argue that the decline in religious belief in Europe since the sixteenth century has in fact been a beneficial liberation from fear and superstition. They see the history of the modern world as one in which the old superstitions of religion were gradually eliminated in favour of the new rational outlook of the European Enlightenment, based on science. This has been a victory for reason over against the reactionary and authoritarian impositions of unquestioning faith.

That is a strange way to look at the history of Europe from the sixteenth to the twentieth centuries. For it was more obviously an age of increasingly aggressive nationalism ending in two world wars, repeated revolutionary conflicts, imperial expansion, the expansion of human slavery to industrial and global proportions, and violent political radicalism set against repressive absolutist monarchies.

It was not an age in which bloody conflicts based on outmoded superstitions were superseded by the calm and peaceable deliberations of rational discourse. It was an age of social revolution, imperial domination and territorial aggression. Science and technology made great advances, but some of these advances were concerned with making more terrifying weapons for war, and enabling Europeans – and later, North Americans – to dominate the world economically and politically.

Old forms of religion, especially those associated with the Holy Roman empire and with the old aristocratic families of Europe, were engulfed in these conflicts. New forms of religion, especially the Protestant Reformation, validated criticisms of traditional church teaching and claimed the right of dissent from established authorities, thereby encouraging political moves to rebel against inherited tradition.

But the rebellion, when it came in France with the fall of the Bastille in 1789, brought with it the guillotine and the Terror, and Napoleon's *coup d'état* to inaugurate a new French empire. There was a feeble attempt to start a 'religion of reason' in France. But Liberty, in Delacroix's famous painting *Liberty on the Barricades*, carried a rifle, and Reason waded in the blood of the thousands who were garrotted and beheaded in her name.

I do not mean to decry the Enlightenment, the importance of freedom of belief and of critical investigation, the growth of scientific understanding and the requirement that all political and moral principles should be justified in some more or less impartial way. But I do mean to throw doubt on any claim that in Europe during these five centuries there was a move from religious superstition to enlightened rationality. Barbarism did not decrease. In the twentieth century it reached heights never previously imaginable. Where religion was restricted, as it was in National Socialist Germany, or even abolished, as it was in revolutionary France and Russia, what superseded it was cruel and inhumane to an unprecedented degree. When there were movements to abolish the slave trade, to establish a Universal Declaration on Human Rights, to limit the arms trade, to call for factory acts and social legislation to alleviate the poverty caused by industrial capitalism, and to criticise violent revolution or indiscriminate bombing of cities, religiously inspired individuals took a leading role. Sir William Wilberforce, Frederick Nolde, Lord Shaftesbury, Bishop Bell, Trevor Huddleston and Martin Luther King are just some of the names of those who have helped to make this a more just and humane world. I do not wish to support the absurd over-simplification: 'religion good; secularism bad'. I simply wish to point out that it is equally absurd to say: 'religion bad; secularism good'. In specific social conditions, secularism can lead to great evil and religion can safeguard good. Perhaps the broadly secular culture of the West would do well to listen to the voices of religion.

Religion and reason

It is entirely plausible to suppose that religion, despite its flaws, has been one of the great humanising movements of recent European history. It was religion, not secular thought, that propounded the view that nature is founded on a deep rationality. Among the greatest defenders of reason in philosophical thought were Anselm and Aquinas, who believed that since God created the universe through the *Logos*, the divine wisdom, the universe must be supremely rational. It is no accident that modern science took root and flourished in a basically Christian society. Copernicus was a lay canon of the Catholic Church. Kepler studied the heavens believing that they manifested the wisdom and beauty of God. Newton formulated the laws of nature in the belief that the wise author of nature must have ordered the cosmos in accordance with rational and comprehensible principles. An important motivating force in science is the belief that there are comprehensible, elegant and mathematically beautiful laws in nature. It did not have to be that way – unless there is a supremely rational creator.

In a sense, much of the Enlightenment was a rejection of the scope and power of reason – its limitation to the subordinate role of rearranging the data provided by the senses, or to being, as David Hume put it, the 'slave of the passions'. So when Enlightenment thought turned to consider social and political issues, it often tended to enthrone passion and desire as the fundamental driving forces of society, and to assign to reason the subordinate role of finding some way of finding a workable compromise between conflicting passions. It is not surprising that the French 'religion of reason' never had any appeal. Who in their right mind would want to worship a slave?

A religious view of society, at least in the Abrahamic traditions, works on the principle that God has created human beings to be free and responsible agents. Presumably God values each thing that is created, and wishes things to flourish as much as possible. God is usually thought to have a special regard for human persons, as beings that can help to work out God's purposes by their own responsible action. So it seems a natural implication of belief in a creator that each person is of value, and that the flourishing and well-being of each person is willed by God. Each person should have the opportunity to realise their own special God-given potentialities in a society where all contribute to the common good.

This is a simple principle. But it contradicts any idea that some people are not worth considering, or that individual well-being is wholly subordinate to the needs of the state. It is a principle that Isaiah Berlin, in his famous essay, 'Two Concepts of Liberty'[1], called 'positive freedom'. This is the freedom positively to realise oneself – and it may well require social legislation to help people to realise their capacities, which they cannot do alone or in conditions of purely voluntary association.

Positive and negative freedom

Berlin contrasted this principle with another principle of freedom, which he called negative freedom — freedom from interference. Negative freedom requires social rules to prevent people interfering with each other in such a way as to infringe a set of negatively defined rights (such as 'do not kill' or 'do not steal'). But it will not positively seek to tell people what desires they should be realising, and how.

This is the principle of what might be called 'negative liberalism': the only justifiable reason for state interference or coercion by others is to prevent the invasion of the minimal rights of others, particularly rights to accumulate property, and to live in reasonable security.

Freedom is not an overriding duty, and it may be overridden by demands of justice, which may limit freedom in the name of equality, for example. Indeed, Berlin points out that negative freedom was hardly mentioned as a virtue before the Reformation. Of course it was always desirable that people should not be enslaved or oppressed by governments, foreign or native. In that sense, freedom from interference has always been a virtue. But Isaiah Berlin suggested that it was perhaps only at the Reformation that the right to dissent and to practise one's own religion and have one's own beliefs became important. In response to what they perceived as the corruption of the church, the Reformers had to insist on the freedom to criticise and to challenge the beliefs of a ruling elite.

The Reformers, however, would hardly have defended pure negative liberalism — the view that all frustration of human desires is wrong, and that non-interference by others is good. They sowed the seeds of liberalism, but they certainly believed that there was a right way of life laid down in the Bible, and they sometimes inclined to enforce it where possible. In Geneva, for instance, John Calvin attempted to cajole or coerce all citizens into living by the presumed laws of God.

However, Protestant Christians also held that faith is a matter of personal commitment, not of birth or some external ceremony like infant baptism. As such, faith cannot logically be coerced, and so in Protestantism there is an inherent drive to full liberty of conscience that made experiments like Calvin's Geneva paradoxical and in the end insupportable.

Freedom of conscience has always been a fundamental principle of Christian thought, though it has often been counterbalanced by paternalistic considerations that the truth must be safeguarded and that evil choices or choices that radically mislead others must be curbed. This sort of paternalism is not just a religious principle. All societies impose some form of censorship, whether on the publication of state secrets, or on pornography, or on the propagation of distortions and lies. The balance between freedom and concern for security or minimal moral standards or truth is a delicate and fluctuating one. What became apparent to many at the Protestant Reformation was that the censoring authority itself had become untrustworthy, and that the freedom to criticise was a condition of truth, not the expression of some perverted moral impulse.

Though, like Isaiah Berlin, I am associating this with sixteenth-century Protestantism, it should be said that the principle of liberty of conscience and religion has always in theory been a key Christian principle, and has been fully affirmed by the Roman Catholic Church at the Second Vatican Council. My concern is simply to say that the modern preference for liberal democratic societies was not forged in opposition to religion as some sort of purely rational principle, overthrowing the authority of blind faith.

The impetus for liberalism had religious roots in a renewed perception, present in the earliest days of Christianity but resurfacing with great force in sixteenth-century Europe, that freedom to dissent from established and enforced beliefs, and freedom to form and express one's own beliefs, was essential to a serious concern with truth, in religion as elsewhere. In a similar way, the movement towards democratic participation in government has deep roots in the Christian belief that all are equal in the sight of God, for all are made 'in the image of God'. And all are called to play their part in caring for the earth and building a just and fair society.

There certainly have been strongly hierarchical religious movements, and English monarchs have claimed to rule by divine right. But within Christianity there are deep elements that subvert all such claims. The Quakers are perhaps best known for their refusal to bow the knee before monarchs, and their insistence that all have equal liberty before God. But in most theistic religions there is a politically subversive strain that calls monarchs to account before God – thereby ruling out absolute monarchy – and that insists on the equal importance of every human life before God. When social conditions permit it, these strains are likely to become important. They may then take form in a positive concept of liberty. This is the idea that all should have freedom and opportunity to realise the positive capacities presumed to have been created in them by God.

The philosopher T. H. Green put it well: 'The idea of true freedom is the maximum of power for all members of human society alike to make the best of themselves'[2]. This involves the idea that every person is important, and should be able to realise their distinctive human and individual dispositions. But there is presupposed here an ideal of self-realisation, which we can discover when we realise that humans are by nature oriented towards the true, the good and the beautiful. And since humans are social beings, all individual fulfilment should be sustained and expanded by a social framework that promotes the goods of sympathy and cooperation in community, and that minimises threats to the moral life. There are two main parts to such a social framework. First, no one should be permitted through circumstances not of their own making to fall below a reasonable degree of health and well-being. Second, a society should be such as to extend the possibilities and opportunities open to its members.

Isaiah Berlin was suspicious of such a 'positive' idea of liberty. He saw it as carrying the implication that there is just one way in which people ought to live, a hierarchy of values that all should accept. It then becomes possible to claim that some group knows what this ideal is, and may then impose it on others as the path to their true positive freedom. Freedom rapidly becomes tyranny, as in Plato's *Republic*, for true freedom is defined as the freedom to live as one ought to live – that is, as others tell you.

It is arguable that this is just what the Roman Catholic Church did when it censored art and literature, suppressed heretical opinions, and enforced adherence to its own creed. The church did this, of course, for the good of souls in its care – just as parents might compel their children to obey their own way of life and teach them their own beliefs, in the belief that it would be good for them. Right up until Pope Pius IX's *Syllabus of Errors* of 1864, the Catholic Church condemned liberalism in favour of its paternalistic belief in its own spiritual and moral authority and duty of pastoral care.

It was not just the church that took this view. Hobbes took it, Hegel took it, many conservative social theorists have taken it, and it is consonant with a belief that a healthy society must be based on shared moral principles; that, as Lord Devlin put it, the law must express and protect basic moral principles.

However, it is quite possible to believe that there is a morally right way to live – that people should develop their capacities for knowledge, creativity and cooperation, and that they should worship the one true God, for example – while not imposing such a belief on others. One can believe in an ethic of self-realisation without insisting that all should be compelled to realise themselves in the same way. Indeed, there are good reasons for thinking that compulsion cannot work in religion, since it leads more to hypocrisy than to genuine faith.

So the Catholic Church, at the Second Vatican Council in

the 1960s, formally stated that 'man's response to God by
faith ought to be free'[3]. 'Everybody must at all times avoid any
action which seems to suggest coercion', and 'the search for
truth must be carried out... by free enquiry... it is by personal
assent that men must adhere to the truth'. There are reasons
internal to religious faith why the negative freedom of humans
not to be coerced against their wills should coexist with a
voluntarily chosen positive freedom to realise human potential
in the pursuit of truth, beauty and goodness.

The rationale of liberalism in religion and politics

But if it is thought that human life has one supreme moral
goal, why should the law, which has a proper concern with
promoting human good, not make it obligatory to hold the
beliefs that are most conducive to that goal? The chief reason
is that justifiable beliefs must be based on evidence or
reasoning, not on custom or judicial decision. Particularly with
the growth of the 'new learning' in the late Middle Ages, it
became evident that custom and tradition were unreliable
guides to truths about the natural world – Aristotle, the
'master of those who know', was wrong in a great deal of what
he said about the natural world. And the church, the guardian
of morality, was seen to be very obviously prone to corruption,
and so probably not the most reliable guide in that area.

When Plato's Guardians are found to be mistaken and
morally corrupt, a social system based on their strong control
loses its justification. What is wrong with paternalism is that
fathers are intellectually and morally imperfect. Growing
children might do well to cast a critical eye over what their
parents tell them, and look elsewhere for confirmation of such
parental advice as they have received.

The lesson of history is that dictators have opinions that
grow weirder as they grow older, and they are apt in the end to
go completely mad. Those who seek to rule are often likely to

be those consumed with ambition and the desire for power. So they will be especially prone to enforce their ideas on others, however odd or idiosyncratic those ideas may be. Most people need to be protected from their rulers, not forced to be obedient to their intellectual whims.

In addition to this, the Reformers discovered, though they did not always admit, that in matters of morality, politics and religion, there are few certainties and many varieties of opinion. What they did admit and proclaim was that the church's beliefs often seemed to be demonstrably different from those that were newly available to all literate people in printed Bibles in the vernacular. Beliefs had changed, sometimes considerably, and authoritarian claims to purvey an unchanging truth came to seem highly questionable. Admittedly the Reformers did not seem to find their own beliefs quite as questionable, but none of us is perfect. What they did find was change, diversity, argument and opinion where what had been claimed was permanence, uniformity, assured revelation and divinely given truth.

God's words may carry absolute certainty, but the opinions of men that God has said certain things should always be viewed with suspicion, or at the very least with less than absolute credulity. Not all such claims can be correct; some are demonstrably mistaken; and there is little reason to believe that rulers, either in church or state, are bound to be right in all they say, even on matters dear to their hearts. The pope may, according to Roman Catholics, be infallible, but he is wise to say as little as possible that might be thought to carry such a portentous property.

The reason that beliefs should not be based simply on authority is that justifiable beliefs should have some stronger basis than that, that authorities are more liable than most people to be tempted to corruptions of power and idiosyncrasy, and that in many important matters, the wide diversity of reasonably argued opinions casts doubt on any particular claim to epistemic certainty.

Plato himself confessed that argument and dialectic are the essence of rational thought, and thus that disagreement is a surer path to truth than dogmatic affirmation. This is true in morals, in aesthetics, in science, in politics and in religion. It is true in most of the important areas of human intellectual life. This is what gives rise to the moderate liberal argument that no beliefs should be imposed on others against their wills, and that there should be liberty of opinion, expression and association.

The price of such liberty is that ideas that are undesirable to most people, or that can seem to some experts to be foolish and rationally unjustifiable, may flourish. When Richard Dawkins visited America, he filmed interviews with some fundamentalist church leaders. Those churches are very successful, sometimes having congregations of thousands. Yet they teach six day creation, which to Dawkins as a biologist seems patently ridiculous and contrary to all that modern science shows to be true. Even if Dawkins is right, however, a liberal attitude would permit the existence of such churches. It would even approve of their attempt to oppose the intellectual dogmas of some modern scientists, on the ground that they might thereby bring to light some overlooked aspect of truth.

The only proper response to such views is to present the evidence and engage in open debate. Dawkins chose to ridicule them instead. Which is the more dangerous: tolerance of and engagement with views you take to be absurd, or the suppression of views that are opposed to what you believe to be certainly true? The latter is the view of the Inquisition. The former is the hard-won consequence of the Reformation acceptance of critical thinking and tolerance of diversity.

Reason, passion and the Enlightenment

In human life there are coercionists and there are liberals. That is true in every area of social life, not just religion. But it is important to see that it was the religious movement of the Reformation that strongly impelled the liberal defence of freedom to dissent. It also helped forward movements towards democratic government, as it rejected ecclesiastical hierarchies, and eventually the social hierarchies with which they were allied in Europe. And it motivated a greater moral concern for equality, as it stressed the value of community in worship and the equality of all in the eyes of God.

I am not pretending that religious beliefs alone gave rise to Enlightenment beliefs in liberty, equality and fraternity. But I am proposing that the basic religious beliefs of the Protestant Reformation positively helped to set in train and motivate the whole complex movement we call the Enlightenment, and the growth of liberal attitudes in religion and politics. Liberalism was not a secular movement that forced religion reluctantly to follow. It was a movement rooted in religious thought, and it is traceable back to the foundational beliefs of the New Testament, which presents Jesus as a religious dissident, executed by the establishment for his radical religious views.

There is a drive towards a secular society in this form of liberalism, in the sense of a society that permits many forms of belief, and does not unduly privilege one of them. The Reformers did not always see that. But this is not a secularism that decries and marginalises religion. It is a society that permits many forms of religion, enjoining only tolerance and mutual acceptance of integrity and conscientiousness.

It is not true that the Enlightenment in Europe was an anti-religious movement, replacing the authoritarian acceptance of religious beliefs with the clear and dispassionate dictates of reason. Quite to the contrary, it is religion that safeguards reason against its critical destruction by the unrestricted scepticism of the radical Enlightenment. The Enlightenment at its best was a call to allow freedom of expression, to encourage informed critical enquiry in every area, including religion, to encourage the growth of experimental science, and to have the courage to follow the dictates of one's own conscience. At its worst, however, it led to the undermining of respect for the uniqueness of human personhood, to denial of the objective authority of morality, to scepticism about reason itself, and to an instrumental attitude to nature which sees it as existing only to fulfil human needs.

There are deep religious motivations to enlarge human freedom, to seek truth by the most effective means, to understand more fully the world God has created, and to ensure that scientific advances do not neglect respect for human personhood or despoil the natural environment. In this sense, religion is a safeguard against the most negative consequences of the Enlightenment heritage. It has the power and the possibility to try to make growing technologies the servants of the needs and potentialities of all humans. Whereas some Enlightenment thinkers sought to make reason the slave of the passions, religious belief should seek to make the passions, which are so often disordered, self-interested and unconcerned with others, not slaves but servants of reason — of a truly disinterested and impartial concern for the greatest possible well-being of all creatures in this rationally ordered and beautiful cosmos that God has created and surely cherishes.

Part Four
Does religion do more harm than good?

Chapter 9
Does religion do more harm than good in personal life?

Questions from psychology

My argument so far has been that belief in God, or in an objective moral ideal, superior to humanity, to which humans can give their undivided loyalty, is perfectly rational. It is not a matter of having deductive proofs or publicly observable evidence – to think that rational belief in God depends on such things is to commit a major category mistake, a mistake of reason. Belief in God, like belief in ultimate moral values, in the uniformity of nature, or in the dignity of human nature, is a foundational belief, a rational postulate that is validated by its ability to provide a workable, fruitful, coherent and comprehensive intellectual account of all the varied experiences and occurrences of human life.

So religious belief can be rational, even if some forms of it are obviously incoherent or morally dubious or incompatible with our general knowledge of the world from other sources. But is religious belief harmful in personal life? I shall consider this question under five main headings. First, does religious belief bring more happiness or more misery to individual human beings? Second, does religious belief lead to greater or to less moral commitment and altruism? Third, is religious belief more associated with mental illness or with mental health and sanity? Fourth, is religious belief merely some form of delusion? And fifth, is religious belief caused by a malfunction of the brain?

Faith and happiness

To answer the first question properly, we would need to ask every believer on earth and examine their behaviour and mental states closely. That is obviously impossible. But what we can do is to take a number of social surveys, which have been accepted by sociologists as having adequate samples and unbiased, cross-checked questions, and which have been analysed and statistically summarised by competent social scientists.

There are in fact many such social surveys that provide data on the perceived relationship between religious commitment and personal happiness. The social psychologist David Myers, author of one of the most widely used introductions to social psychology in the United States, has usefully surveyed a number of them in his forthcoming book *The Science of Subjective Well-Being*[1].

He cites a Gallup survey from 1984 on religion in America, which concludes that spiritually committed people (people who agree that God is very important in their lives) are twice as likely to report being 'very happy' than the least religiously committed people (people who do not regard God as important to them).

He also cites data from the National Opinion Research Center and from the Pew organisation, which report the same conclusion. In 2003, Smith, McCullough and Poll carried out an analysis of over 200 social studies, and found that high religiousness (at least weekly church or synagogue attendance) predicts a rather lower risk of depression and drug abuse and fewer suicide attempts, and more reports of satisfaction with life and a sense of well-being. In 2002 Bryan Johnson and colleagues of the University of Pennsylvania Center for Research on Religion and Urban Civil Society reviewed 498 studies that had been published in peer-reviewed journals. They concluded that a large majority of studies showed a positive correlation between religious commitment and higher

levels of perceived well-being and self-esteem, and lower levels
of hypertension, depression and criminal delinquency.

A standard reference text in the field is the *Handbook of
Religion and Health*, edited by Harold Koenig, Michael
McCullough and David Larson[2]. The authors review 2,000
published experiments designed to test the relationship
between religion and various medical conditions such as heart
disease, cancer and depression. Yet again the overall result is
that religious people tend to live longer and physically
healthier lives than those who are non-religious. Young
religious people have significantly lower levels of drug and
alcohol abuse, criminal delinquency and attempted suicide.
Older religious people have a stronger sense of well-being and
life satisfaction. Insofar as any general remarks are in order in
this area, religion is good for your health!

It may be said that this is just an American phenomenon,
where it is already believed that religion is supposed to make
you happy, so the results are not too surprising. But social
surveys in Britain, when they ask such questions, turn up
similar results. Even in China, an officially non-religious
country where religion was banned for many years, a recent
survey carried out by Xinzhong Yao and Paul Badham for the
Ian Ramsey Centre at Oxford University, reported that while
only 8.7 per cent of interviewees (all Han Chinese) described
themselves as religious – hardly surprising in an officially
atheistic state – an amazing 56.7 per cent confirmed they had
experience of a spiritual being or power. Of those, 15 per cent
believed their experience made their psychological condition
better, while 7 per cent thought their moods were made worse.
Overall, positive experiences such as guiding or inspiring or
blessing formed a much higher proportion of the reported
responses than negative feelings of fear or terror.

It seems that religious experiences are quite widespread,
though not universal. And they are largely beneficial to
happiness and health, though again not universally so.
Obviously there are cases where religion does not bring

happiness. A lot will depend upon the society in which people live, and upon the particular sort of religion they encounter. Many authors have written about their own feelings of guilt and fear, produced by some form of religious upbringing. Perhaps it was their propensity to have such feelings that turned them into authors, a notoriously unstable breed. It is obviously not true that religion always produces happiness, and no responsible investigator would claim that it does. But when these surveys — and many like them in all countries where social surveys exist — are taken into account, it becomes clear that religion is not founded, as David Hume claimed, on fear and terror. On the contrary, the relation of most religious people to their gods is one that is positive, and increases happiness and a sense of security.

This finding is enough to disprove any contention that religion mostly preys on fear and guilt, and causes people to feel insecure and to have low self-esteem. Some forms of religious belief or practice may do so, but there is a greater overall correlation between religious commitment, health and happiness.

David Myers points out that there may be many explanations for this fact. Religious affiliation usually provides a strong degree of social support. Where belief is sincere, it gives a sense of something of great value, worth giving one's whole life to, and thus increases a sense of purpose and meaning. Most religious beliefs are good for self-esteem, teaching for example that we are loved by God. They provide an ultimate hope that can survive almost any present suffering and make it more bearable. And they reinforce a number of positive social virtues, such as humility, forgiveness and gratitude.

All these things help towards having a happy, satisfactory or fulfilled life. This does not show that religious beliefs are true. But it does show that at least in this respect religion is in general beneficial to happiness. It is far from being an illness or a disabling factor in human life.

It is important to identify forms of religion that are disabling or that bring misery or fear. The best way to remedy them is not to eliminate all religion, but to counter them with a clearer perception of what good religion really is – the disciplined cultivation of relationship with superior and beneficent spiritual powers (for monotheists, with God) that promise human happiness as a worthwhile goal.

Faith and altruism

I conclude that religious belief is, on balance, good for human happiness and well-being. It is not usually the cause of misery, depression, guilt and anxiety. A distinction should probably be made between negative and positive religious beliefs. Then the evidence suggests that, while negative religious beliefs exist, most religious beliefs are perceived as positive, and overall religious belief is a positive factor in human happiness and well-being. This makes it very important to analyse and distinguish positive and negative religious beliefs rather carefully. In the main religious traditions, the crucial texts almost always stress the positive beliefs – the joy of God's presence and the happiness of obeying the divine will. In view of this, the most pressing programme for religion today is to seek the causes of negative beliefs and ways to counteract them. Because of human evil and irrationality, this will never be completely achieved. But by working closely with psychologists, sociologists and those who make public policy, much that is positive can and should be done.

Concentration on the links between religion and happiness may have a slightly self-centred feel. What about the effects of religion on people's moral outlooks and behaviour? Does religious belief tend to make people more or less altruistic? That is the second question to be addressed.

In this area, too, there is a great deal of published material from social surveys, and any serious investigation of the question – any one that even pretends to adopt a scientific approach – must begin with them.

The sociologist Gordon Allport, reporting a number of surveys on moral and religious attitudes in 1958, commented that religion had a paradoxical role in this area. On the one hand American church members showed more racial prejudice than non-churchgoers. Churchgoers tended to be more conservative in their moral and political attitudes in general (in other words, to be Republicans rather than Democrats). David Myers points out that the incidence of racial prejudice was lower among regular attenders than among nominal members, and that clergy were more supportive of civil rights movements than laity. Indeed there was obviously a very strong religious component among civil rights leaders such as Martin Luther King. So the paradox is that those who said they were religious believers in general were rather more racially prejudiced, while a smaller number of more religiously committed believers were among the most active people seeking to overcome racial prejudice.

The same pattern was found under the South African regime of Apartheid, when members of the Dutch Reformed Church were mostly in favour of racial separation, yet very prominent in the anti-Apartheid movement were church leaders such as Trevor Huddlestone and Desmond Tutu.

Religion can serve as a reinforcer of conservative social attitudes, especially for nominal members of religious groups. But a number of those who take religion very seriously often take very radical social attitudes. Sir William Wilberforce was aroused by his religious convictions to oppose the slave trade in Britain in the eighteenth century. In the nineteenth century the Earl of Shaftesbury was led by his Christian beliefs to reform the factories and mines of Britain and to improve provisions for mental health. As John Nurser shows in detail in his book, *For All Peoples and All Nations*[3], a number of committed Christians – especially the American Lutheran Frederick Nolde – worked in the 1940s to construct and press for a United Nations declaration of Human Rights. This historical declaration was adopted in 1948 and has become a model for further declarations and conventions on rights throughout the world. And, to the surprise of many, legislation permitting divorce and remarriage was advocated in the English parliament by the bishops of the Anglican Church.

When examined more closely, it is not after all a paradox that when religion has been a stabilising social force for some time, it will reinforce generally conservative attitudes. But when new perceptions of what justice requires emerge, serious reflection on religious values such as justice and compassion will lead some believers to play leading roles in movements for reform. It is not the case that religious believers are always on the conservative side and opposed to reform. The true picture is more complex: religion in general exerts a conservative influence in many respects, but committed belief can inspire outstanding courage and radical action when perceived injustice becomes apparent.

If the picture is complex with regard to levels of prejudice and conservatism, it is much clearer in other morally relevant areas. American social surveys show that engagement in volunteer work with the socially underprivileged or the sick is strongly correlated with levels of religious commitment. A Gallup survey in 1984 in America reported that 46 per cent of committed believers engaged in volunteer work, whereas 22 per cent of those with no religious affiliation did so. A General Social Survey in the United States in 1995 recorded that community service was felt to be an important obligation by 40 per cent of weekly attenders of religious organisations, as opposed to 19 per cent of non-attenders, who felt there was no such obligation.

It must be borne in mind that this implies that 60 per cent of weekly religious attenders did not think that community service was an important obligation. So it is not true that most religious believers support community service. We can always find plenty who do not. However, it is true that many more believers than non-believers are committed to thinking that community service is a good thing. Even though most religious believers are not discernibly morally committed in these respects, nevertheless religious belief is in general a positive force for moral commitment.

Of course, such surveys only record what people say in answer to questions, but a survey by Robert Putnam in 2000 of 200 volunteer organisations showed that membership of religious groups was positively correlated with membership of the volunteer organisations. It seems incontrovertible that religious commitment correlates highly with community service – that is, with an altruistic rather than a self-centred attitude to life.

With regard to charitable giving, Gallup in 1992 reported that the religiously committed (24 per cent of the surveyed population) gave 48 per cent of charitable contributions. Many other surveys reinforce this finding. So the general effect of religious belief is to increase both participation in charitable work and giving to charitable organisations. This has to be seen as a positive link between religion and altruistic behaviour.

That is not surprising, since religion survives at least in part because it has contributed to social utility, and as such it strengthens both strong in-group bias and tendencies to altruistic behaviour. If evolutionary psychologists are right, it is to be expected that it would also raise the probability of out-group hostility and suspicion of outsiders. The combination of a degree of out-group intolerance and a much larger degree of limited altruism is just what one would expect from a successful social institution. The interesting thing it shows is that religion is a useful moral reinforcer, and as such it is – as the founding father of sociology, Emile Durkheim, always argued that it was – an invaluable moral tool.

Naturally we would wish to decrease the force of out-group intolerance and encourage more universal altruistic tendencies. As I have argued in previous chapters, responsible religious teachings seek to do this. But religion has to work with human nature as it actually is. The evidence from social psychology is that religious belief functions in general to increase group solidarity and altruism, and that it often reinforces prejudice against and intolerance of groups perceived as hostile – but also that committed, as opposed to nominal, believers are often active in seeking to counteract such negative tendencies. The evidence does not show that religion is wholly beneficial. But it does show that religious belief is positively correlated with a greater degree of altruistic behaviour, even if such altruism is often limited in extent. In a world that is very morally ambiguous and often dominated by greed and selfishness, religion is a positive force for altruism, and at least in theory it seeks to extend such altruism beyond the bounds of race and creed.

Marxist suggestions that religion is just a force for preserving social inequalities and keeping the impoverished happy with the thought of a reward after death for their present misery are not supported by these data. Ironically, the Marxist theory was undermined most spectacularly in Poland, when Communism itself was the tyranny against which the Catholic underground movement Solidarity pitted itself. Religious believers were able to overthrow one of the most repressive social regimes in history just by the power of active faith, a faith that inspired a strong and often self-sacrificial commitment to social justice.

For a properly scientific study of religion much more work is needed. But the results of social surveys to date show a correlation between certain sorts of religious and moral commitment. Naturally, if a person happens not to agree with the moral views that some religious believers hold, that person will not regard this as a wholly good thing. On other moral topics, no such correlation is apparent. Moral views are very divided on issues such as homosexuality and genetic engineering. The possibly surprising fact is that religious believers are as divided on these issues as is the population in general. Social surveys on values show a complete division of opinion in the general population of European countries on the issue of homosexuality and on the permissibility of genetic experimentation. For example, the European Values Study[4], monitored by Tilburg University in the Netherlands, is the most authoritative research project on these topics. In the 1990 survey, on a scale of 1 to 10, permissiveness with regard to homosexual practice varied from 1.5 in Azerbaijan to 7.8 in the Netherlands. These statistics do not correlate with degrees of religious commitment, but they show how very varied and opposed attitudes to homosexual practice are in general populations. It is false to think that secularists favour homosexuality and religious believers oppose it. It seems that religious belief is not, contrary to widespread legend, and even contrary to official pronouncements by some conservative religious bodies, a very significant indicator of opinion in these areas.

Thus on controversial moral issues, religious belief and practice tends to reflect more general social trends. When it comes to altruism in general, however, religion unequivocally favours and encourages altruistic behaviour.

It must be kept in mind that what we are talking about here are correlations, not tight logical connections. It is not being argued that all religious believers will be more altruistic than all atheists. Obviously you are going to be able to find lots of believers who are not very altruistic. It is just that many more believers than unbelievers will be altruistic.

I am not arguing that believers are 'morally better' than unbelievers. What I am saying, and what the data support, is that taken overall, and other things being equal, religious belief is a strong support for moral and altruistic behaviour. Surveys also show that religious belief is to some degree correlated with higher levels of intolerance or prejudice. This is, as Bernard Spilka and his co-authors say in *The Psychology of Religion*[5], an uncomfortable fact that religions need to come to terms with and to try to counteract. We can see more clearly now that religions are not wholly and unambiguously forces for good. But taking all the available evidence into account, it is not true that religion is actually a force for evil or social disintegration. Its drawbacks and disadvantages are just those that evolutionary psychology might lead us to expect of a social institution that has been beneficial in the long term for most societies. There are ways in which many aspects of religion still need to be reformed. But far from being socially harmful, religion has played and continues to play a vital and desirable role in human society.

Faith and mental illness

The third question I posed was whether religion is associated with mental illness of some sort – whether it is, for example, as Freud once suggested, a form of 'obsessional neurosis'. There are data relevant to this question, and the answer they give is a pretty resounding 'No!'.

The Oxford psychologist Michael Argyle spent many years investigating the question of whether religious belief correlates with any identifiable psychiatric illness, or indeed with any particular sort of psychological personality type. In *Psychology and Religion*[6], he surveys many sets of psychological tests, and concludes that there is no positive correlation between any one personality type and religious belief. In *Religious Behaviour*[7], he analyses data obtained both from social surveys and from clinical psychiatric reports in the United States and in Britain between 1900 and 1957. He emphasises that such surveys need to adopt some sort of definition of 'religiousness' – usually church-going or positive responses to questions about the importance of God in one's life. These surveys are limited to fairly liberal, partly secular and partly Christian societies. And they can give at best a number of statistical correlations, without being able to say definitively whether, for example, religiosity is caused by conservative personality traits or vice versa. So they cannot be treated as providing universal and indisputable conclusions. Nevertheless, the data are treated in a dispassionate way, and have been closely scrutinised by scholars with many religious beliefs and none. They are the best data we have, and while we must be cautious not to overgeneralise, they are sufficient to undermine any general thesis that religious belief is some sort of psychological pathology or malfunction.

Generally speaking, a psychosis is a clinical condition such as schizophrenia, paranoia or epilepsy. Some writers have proposed a connection between schizophrenia, epilepsy and religiosity. In schizophrenia, patients feel that thoughts are put into their minds. They hear voices and have delusions. Their thought patterns are typically vague and illogical. In extreme cases, they become apathetic, eccentric and isolated personalities. It is estimated that about 1 per cent of all known populations suffer from this condition, 'regardless of language, creed or social structure'[8]. This already implies that religiosity is not a major causal factor in schizophrenia.

Farr and Howe[9] record that 13 per cent of 500 mental patients, or about 1 in 7, had 'definite religious content' to their illness. That means, of course, that the vast majority of psychoses, 6 out of 7, were not discernibly religious. Fleck, in 1935, claimed that of 157 epileptic patients only 20 per cent had a positive conformist attitude to religion[10]. Quite a few, but only a minority, of epileptic patients have 'religious' symptoms. In a more recent study, Ogata and Myakawa[11] state that only 3 out of 234 patients with temporal lobe epilepsy reported religious content during seizures. And Penfield and Jaspers, in a classic study of temporal lobe epilepsy[12], record no cases of religious hallucinations at all. David Tucker and colleagues, in 1987, state that 'hyper-religiosity is not a consistent interictal [sic] trait of individuals with temporal lobe epilepsy'[13].

Among mental patients, schizophrenic patients have more religious delusions, or show unduly serious concern with 'ultimate questions' more often, than other patients. This does not show that religion causes schizophrenia. It shows that religion might, in psychiatric terms, be pathoplastic rather than psychogenic – that is, religious ideas may provide a handy content for schizophrenic disorder, without being the cause of the disorder.

W. Oates, in the *Journal for Pastoral Care*[14], estimates that about 20 per cent of religious psychotics (a minority group of psychotics) had religion as a precipitating cause of illness. Some 35 per cent had family or social conflicts over religion as a precipitating cause. And 45 per cent had religious symptoms, but the causes did not seem to be themselves religious. H. J. Cronin, on the other hand, in the *Medical Review*[15], decided that religion was not the precipitating cause for any of his neurotic patients. It is obviously easier to note correlations than to assign the real causes of behaviour. But whatever the difficulties of interpretation, there is little or no positive evidence that religion is a major cause or symptom of mental illness.

This may suggest that if a religious person is going to be mentally ill, their illness will display religious features. But there are many people who show an unduly serious concern with ultimate questions who are not mentally ill at all. They are called philosophers. And groups of religious believers can usually pick out those of their members who show symptoms, usually quite mild, of obsessive or neurotic personality.

One problem is that the cases that gain most publicity are those in which some religious leader is obviously suffering from paranoia or schizophrenia, yet becomes accepted as a leader by many devotees. This may give the impression that in some way religious leadership is connected with mental illness. But a calmer study of the archbishop of Canterbury, the pope, the supreme primate of Japanese Pure Land Buddhism, and the majority of religious leaders throughout the world, will reveal that, while they may all wear funny hats and perform peculiar ceremonies from time to time, they are not actually mentally ill.

The conclusion is that most schizophrenics are not

religious, and most religious people are not schizophrenic. As Michael Argyle puts it, 'There is little evidence that religion ever causes mental disorders – apart from the states temporarily induced in hysterics by revivals – or that religion prevents disorders. Although young religious people have an above-average tendency to be neurotic, and psychotic patients often have religious ideas, these religious symptoms may be projections of deeper conflicts'[16].

There is, then, no evidence that religion is a sort of mental illness, that it is a significant cause of mental illness, or that religious believers have a higher incidence of mental illness than other social groups. On the contrary, it is clear that most mental illness is physical or neurological in origin, and as such it is not under the patients' voluntary control. However, insofar as religion is in general conducive to a sense of health and well-being, religion is to be commended for its positive psychological effects.

This has been increasingly recognised in recent years, and Professor Andrew Sims, former president of the Royal College of Psychiatrists in Britain, said, 'Rather belatedly, the Royal College of Psychiatrists has recognised the need to consider spiritual issues'[17], and seen the need to train psychiatrists in the spiritual aspects of healing. Far from religion being a form of mental illness, it is increasingly acknowledged that it may play a positive part in personal well-being.

For religious believers, two very important points emerge from these studies. One is that mental illness should never be confused with spiritual failure or lack of faith. It is largely based on, and caused by, physical malfunctions of the brain. The other is that a positive relationship to God should, illness aside, be conducive to human well-being and happiness. Religion does not exist in order to make people healthy. It exists to liberate human lives from evil and relate them to a reality of supreme wisdom, compassion and bliss. It should not be considered as a magical substitute for medical care in cases of illness. But overall it is a positive contributor to mental health.

In both these respects, psychology can be very helpful to religious belief. It can clarify the neurophysiological basis of conscious feelings and experiences. And it can help people to become aware of their own personality type and dispositions, and to take steps, where that is possible, to counteract negative dispositions.

Faith and delusion

There are some religious people who have very odd beliefs. There are people, religious and non-religious, who claim to have been given secret information about the meaning of life, who feel impelled to devote their lives to some utterly useless activity, or who think they are extra-terrestrial walk-ins. I used to worry about this, until I talked to a colleague of mine who is a professor of physics. He told me that he receives about three letters a week from people who have disproved Einstein's theory of relativity, or who have solved the problems of quantum physics – though strangely enough no one will listen to them, and there is usually a conspiracy to prevent their articles from being published.

That cheered me up considerably. It is not just religious people who are odd. Most people seem to be odd, in one way or another. People suffer delusions and hallucinations, they hear voices and see visions, they know about conspiracies and have insight into secret truths.

The fact is that psychiatrists have ways of distinguishing religious paranoia from ordinary religious belief, and they are aware that paranoia is not necessarily religious – though religion provides quite a handy home for paranoid ideas, if only because the religious are slightly more tolerant and tend to listen to weird ideas more sympathetically than most people.

It is even less plausible to say that religious belief is, as such, a delusion. A delusion is defined by the *Oxford Companion to*

Mind as 'a fixed, idiosyncratic belief, unusual in the culture to which the person belongs'. It is a clearly false opinion, especially as a symptom of a mental illness. Not all false opinions are delusions. I may think that the speed of light is 1,000 miles per second. That is false. We might call it a mistake, but we would not call it a delusion. A delusion is a belief so obviously false that all reasonable people would see it to be mistaken – like John Smith thinking that he is Jesus. We need to have a special explanation for why people should have such delusions. A delusion is an irrational belief. So if I think I am Napoleon, that is a delusion. All reasonable people would see that I am wrong, and I could only explain the belief by some inability of mine to form a rational estimate of my social position. Further, if I am delusional I will react to criticism of my belief with excessive anger and total resistance to disconfirming evidence.

Belief in God is very different. Most great philosophers have believed in God, and they are reasonable people. It can be a diverting pastime to ask what mental illness different classical philosophers must have been suffering from. Perhaps Bishop Berkeley, who believed matter did not exist, suffered from excessive potty-training. Or maybe Immanuel Kant, who thought that space and time were imposed by the mind onto reality, had delusions of grandeur. But these are not serious exercises in psychology. The line between crazy notions and brilliant ideas may be thin, but it exists. On which side of the line does the idea of God lie? Or on which side of the line does atheism lie? It does not seem as though either is actually crazy, even though some very odd people expound them.

In any case, how is mental illness to be defined? The UK Mental Health act of 1959 defines a psychopathic personality as one with 'a persistent disorder or disability of the mind… which results in abnormally aggressive or seriously irresponsible conduct… and is susceptible to medical treatment'. In general, a mental illness is something that makes oneself or others suffer. A mentally ill person is unable to carry out the everyday tasks of life efficiently. They cannot engage in normal social relationships, or relate to other people in normal ways.

To act normally is to be able to give reasons for one's actions that would be generally acceptable, and could be seen to be relevant to the sort of action in question. So to eat because I am hungry is reasonable. But if I eat compulsively, far beyond the requirements of survival, so that there are bad effects on my health and social life, that may be pathological.

Some religious acts, like the performance of certain rituals, may be compulsive, and may have unwanted social effects if that performance prevents me from having a normal social life. But if I am happy with my compulsion there may be no need for medical intervention. The reasons I give for my repetition of ritual may be unconvincing to others – what does it matter what order I light candles in? But a moderately liberal view will accept that people assess reasons differently, and so will accept that some people may have reasons that others can understand, but not accept. There is nothing wrong as such with loving ritual performances and wanting to see them performed properly. Such behaviour becomes obsessive only when it begins to cause severe anxiety, excessive emotional outbursts and the inability to relate normally to other people.

So the general criteria of mental illness are inability to function normally and inability to provide reasons for action that seem relevant to most people. There is a degree of convention about this – what is 'normal' may vary from one society to another, and what seems 'reasonable' is also not an objectively assessable property.

In some Communist states, it may be abnormal and unreasonable to be religious, and being religious may be harmful to one's prospects of a happy life. It is possible that in such states religious belief is considered suitable for treatment, and believers may be incarcerated in mental institutions. It has happened.

But such societies are rightly called repressive by more liberal states where diversity of opinion is accepted as part of the human condition, and where people are not quite so dogmatically confident that they are right and everybody else is so wrong that they need to be treated rather than argued with.

All that is needed to refute the claim that religious belief is a delusion is one clear example of someone who exhibits a high degree of rational ability, who functions well in the ordinary affairs of life, whose faith seems to enable them to live well and be happy, and who can produce a reasonable and coherent defence of their beliefs. There are thousands of religious believers who are like that, including some of the most able philosophers and scientists in the world today – Alvin Plantinga, Richard Swinburne, Basil Mitchell, Chris Isham, John Barrow, John Polkinghorne. And that is an almost random selection from a very long list indeed. You could hardly ask for a stronger refutation of the argument that religion is a delusion than this.

Of course, not all philosophers and scientists have religious beliefs. One of the things they would all assert is that rational people should expect differences of opinion in religion. They would be very surprised if there were no such differences, and exceedingly surprised if the truth was so obvious that all sensible people agreed.

It is a mark of rationality that we accept that many of our most important beliefs will be contestable. This is true of many beliefs in ethics, in politics, in history, in philosophy, in our views of human nature, as well as in attitudes to religion. It is a sign of irrationality if someone refuses to accept such diversity of opinion, and insists that their own view is just obviously true to everyone – despite the obvious evidence to the contrary.

If someone is very selective in their presentation of evidence, if they refuse to attend seriously to scientific studies of the subject they are talking about, and if they regard everyone who disagrees with them as insane, deluded or irrational, that is itself a mark of irrationality — or at least of a closed mind that finds it impossible to adopt a dispassionate and balanced view of a subject. There are such people in the world, but they are not all religious by any means.

Faith as a brain malfunction

There is one more question arising from modern study of the brain that needs to be addressed. It has sometimes been suggested that religiosity is, if not actually a mental illness, at least a by-product of brain activity that produces illusions that were useful survival mechanisms earlier in human prehistory, but are now apt to be counter-productive.

Recent advances in brain scanning techniques have enabled neuroscientists to map which parts of the brain are active when various conscious processes are taking place, and to show that brain malfunctions produce a range of predictable conscious states and behaviour. Work with PET (position emission tomography) scans and MRI (magnetic resonance imaging) has produced some surprising results. For example, it turns out that many different parts of the brain are active in visual perception, and these different areas are somehow coordinated (but apparently not by any specific area of the brain) to produce the conscious experience of seeing and recognising something. The now famous case of Phineas Gage shows that social conventions and moral rules can be forgotten as a result of brain damage. The unfortunate Mr Gage was a railroad foreman in New England who, in 1848, had part of his brain removed by an iron bar that went clean through his skull. Amazingly, he remained conscious, but thereafter his personality changed, making him apparently indifferent to moral and social considerations. This was obviously caused by the loss of some specific brain functions.

In less spectacular cases, most of us are aware how Alzheimer's dementia, which is caused by observable brain deterioration, brings on loss of memory, confusion and inability to recognise people.

For reasons like these, most neuroscientists are now reluctant to speak of mental illness as something quite distinct from physical illness, as though one belonged to a wholly different realm from the other. They are interested to explore the physical bases of mental illness in the brain, and modern techniques are helping them to do so. It has been discovered, for example, that the controlled use of drugs can often relieve clinical depression, and so it seems that such conditions are due to physical causes in the brain, not to some sort of spiritual malaise.

Some scientists get overexcited by these discoveries. Francis Crick, in his book *The Astonishing Hypothesis*[18] proposes that 'you, your joys and your sorrows, your memories and your ambitions, your sense of personal identity and free will, are in fact *no more than* the behaviour of a vast assembly of nerve cells and their associated molecules' (italics mine). He admits that this hypothesis goes well beyond any available empirical evidence, but is a postulate, acceptance of which could bring great gains in human understanding – it is remarkably like a religious hypothesis, in fact. But if Crick's hypothesis were true, it would show the religious hypothesis to be false.

Suppose Crick said, 'Your belief that $2 + 2 = 4$ is no more than nerve-cell behaviour,' you might well feel that there is at least one thing more to it – namely that the belief is true. If I had the belief that $2 + 2 = 5$, that would also be nerve-cell behaviour. But it would be false. Some nerve-cell behaviour corresponds to the facts, to what is the case in reality, and other behaviour does not. You cannot tell which is which from examining brain activity alone. It is because you know some mathematical truths that you would call the belief that $2 + 2 = 5$ a delusion, and try if you could to repair the brain defect that caused it.

Now take the case of someone who believes in God. Do they have some brain defect, some overactivity of the temporal lobe perhaps, that causes this belief to appear? Well, it would only be a defect if the belief was false. Brain activity that produces the true belief that there is a God would be normal and healthy.

Crick's hypothesis is caused by brain activity, just as belief in God is. As brain activity, there is nothing to choose between them. So how do we know which is true? By reasoned argument, of course, not by further investigation of the brain. The conclusion has to be that Crick's hypothesis cannot be supported by scientific study of the brain. It is a philosophical theory, of a rather crude sort (any theory that contains the words 'no more than' is pretty crude).

What does scientific study of the brain show, then? It shows the physical basis of the beliefs, feelings, experiences and thoughts that we have. It shows that, if you change that physical structure, whether by drugs or by surgery, you will change some beliefs and feelings. That is not altogether surprising – after all, if you cut someone's head off, they will stop having any beliefs at all. What it does not show is which beliefs and feelings we should change, or whether we should do so by artificial means at all.

Malcolm Jeeves, former chair of the International Neuropsychological Symposium and Professor of Psychology at St Andrews University, has written a splendid book on these issues called *Human Nature*[19], and has edited another volume[20] which contains papers by eminent neurologists, psychologists and theologians exploring the relation of mind and brain from a scientific point of view.

General psychiatric opinion is that you should modify beliefs and feelings only if they are seriously harmful, seem clearly irrational, and make it hard for a person to live a normal life in society. I have shown that most religious beliefs do not fall into this category. On the contrary, they can be supported by sophisticated reasoning, they are conducive to mental health, and they are socially beneficial.

Some religious beliefs may be seriously harmful, and we might consider treating those medically, if we consider that the person whose beliefs they are is unable to take responsibility for their own lives or has clearly false beliefs (such as being Napoleon or Jesus).

So what should we say of the view taken by some that religious experiences can be produced by electrically stimulating the brain, or by taking drugs like Mescalin?

Rational religious believers should say that being religious is not just a matter of having ecstatic experiences. In fact it very rarely is that. Being religious, like being scientific, involves having a whole interconnected network of beliefs – about the primacy of spiritual reality, the objectivity of goodness, the importance of moral obligation and the possibility of human fulfilment – that may or may not produce experiences of some describable sort. Believers may indeed hope to apprehend God, but the forms such apprehension may take are various, and, if taken out of their context of beliefs, likely to be spurious.

What neuroscience can do, then, is to clarify the physical basis in the brain of human beliefs and feelings. That is exceptionally important, for it means that personality traits or pathological behaviours may have a physical basis. They are things we need to take into account or possibly modify, but not things for which we are responsible. This will help to clarify the extent and the limits of human freedom and responsibility.

What neuroscience cannot do is prove that religious belief or behaviour is nothing more than a by-product of brain behaviour or of our naturally evolved cognitive processes. The question of truth remains primary.

May nearly universal tendencies to believe in a supernatural reality not have survived precisely because they reflect truth? Brain processes come up with truths and falsehoods. But brain processes alone cannot distinguish between them. What can? People with brains can, and they can do so by using their brains, not by being controlled by them!

Moreover, evolutionary psychology – the explanation of present beliefs and behaviour traits by showing their fitness for survival in the past – does not support the view that consciousness is nothing more than physical brain behaviour. Quite the reverse. As the immunologist and Nobel Laureate Gerald Edelman says, 'The evolutionary assumption [that consciousness conferred fitness]…implies that consciousness is efficacious – that it is not an epiphenomenon'[21]. Consciousness and rationality add new causal factors to the human situation, and though consciousness is an emergent reality, closely dependent upon neurological brain states, it is also a new causal element that has 'downward' effects on the whole brain–body system. In particular, consciousness assigns truth to certain propositions. It is an entirely plausible hypothesis that humans assign truth to propositions about the existence of a God because they provide the basis of the most coherent, fruitful and adequate holistic interpretation of the data of human experience. It is not the case that people believe some religious statements to be true because they were once evolutionarily fit. Rather, evolutionary fitness is much more likely to be a symptom and consequence of the perception of truth.

In summary, religious belief, as far as empirical investigations can go, is good for mental health and for social commitment to altruism. It has little or no positive correlation with any particular personality type or form of mental illness. And while, like all human beliefs, there are physical states of the brain that are necessary to the formation of such beliefs, it is not possible to reduce beliefs to brain states. Religious beliefs may be caused by brain states, like all our other beliefs, and still be true, like many of our other beliefs. In fact, it seems that if we have healthy, normally functioning brains we will tend to believe in God, since the tendency to form such a belief has probably been genetically programmed into our brains. That, it seems to me, is a pretty good indication of truth, and is just what the believer might expect if human brains have, after all, been created by God.

Social surveys can give only statistical correlations, and we may not wish to put too much emphasis on them. But they are the only empirical data we have in the study of religion. And at the very least what they show is that there is no evidence for claiming that religion is founded psychologically on fear, pathological concern with what happens after death, or mental illness. As far as these data show, the influence of religion on personal life, while it may in many cases be bad, is overall and in general good. When considering a phenomenon as complex as human life, one cannot hope for much more.

Chapter 10
What good has religion done?

On condemning religion

I have examined the evidences provided by history, philosophy, psychology and sociology, to see whether they support the view that religion is a dangerous force that humans would be better off without. The evidence seems to me pretty clear that while there are many dangers in religion, overall it is a force for good. I will conclude by asking what positive reasons there are for thinking that religion is good. After all, it has been said that religion is one of the most destructive forces in human life. Hatred, violence, intolerance and bigotry are sustained and inflamed by religious propaganda. The reputation of Christianity was shattered long ago by the Crusades and the Inquisition. The reputation of Islam has been shattered by Islamic terrorist organisations around the globe. Even Hinduism, once naively thought to be a universally tolerant faith, destroys mosques and murders non-Hindus in the name of its own religious culture. Might we not be better off in a world without religion?

This argument may seem strong. But consider a parallel case: politics could also be said to be one of the most destructive forces in human life. In Russia and Cambodia, millions of people have been killed in the name of socialist political ideologies. In Latin America, millions of people 'disappeared' in ruthless campaigns of violence propagated by right-wing politicians. Deception, hypocrisy and misrepresentation are commonplace in political life. Might we not be better off in a world without politics too?

Even science, often thought of as an uninterested search for truth, produces terrifying weapons of mass destruction, and the most advanced technology is used to destroy human lives in ever more effective and brutal ways. Would we be better off without science as well?

The point should be clear: we need to distinguish. Politics, science and religion are necessary to human life. Humans need some form of social organisation. They need to understand and control their environment and they need some sense of ultimate value and meaning to give significance to their existence. Some religious and political forms, just like some scientific inventions, are good, and some are very bad indeed – it all depends on how they are used. It is pointless to condemn politics or science because they are so widely misused; instead, it is necessary to ensure that they are used for good. Similarly, it is pointless to condemn religion, because religion is not the cause of hatred and violence. It can be used to inspire hatred, but it can also be used to inspire heroic love and commitment. The world would be much poorer without Martin Luther King, Gandhi and Mother Teresa; without Mozart, Bach, Rubens and Michelangelo; without St Francis, Siddartha Gautama and Jesus.

The world faiths

I have, I hope, shown how difficult it is to define religion, and how misleading it is to suggest that all religions are basically the same. Nevertheless, throughout the world there are many sets of beliefs and practices whose primary concern is to relate humans to a spiritual being, in a conscious way, for the sake of obtaining good and avoiding harm. This can be taken as a helpful working definition of religion. The *character* of religion, however, depends on what its adherents believe to be good and on what they think the spiritual order is. If I think the good is what benefits my friends and harms my enemies, and that spiritual reality is terrifying as well as powerful, my religion may be pretty dangerous. But if I come to think that the good is what enables all sentient beings to flourish, and that spiritual reality is supremely beautiful, wise and compassionate, my religion can be a tremendous force for human good.

What humans need, therefore, is not the end of religion, but a developed conception of goodness and a deepening perception of the spiritual as the realm of the supremely good. As the world religions evolved, they formed such a conception of one being or state of supreme goodness in conscious relation to which true human fulfilment was to be found. In the main world traditions, this conception took various forms.

(a) Judaism

In the Semitic or Abrahamic traditions, it took the form of one merciful and loving God. We can read in the Hebrew Bible how ideas of God developed as human perceptions of what morality requires deepened. The God of the major prophets of Israel and Judah, of the eighth to the sixth centuries BCE, was a creator of the whole universe with a moral goal for human beings on this planet. That goal was the shaping of societies in which justice and peace would reign, and each individual human would find fulfilment in a harmonious and beneficent community. For the prophets, there are two main goals of religion. One is the worship of God – which basically means contemplation of and reverence for the beauty and perfection of the creator of all things. This involves having love and respect for creation because it is made and valued by God. The other is striving for the 'kingdom of God', the shaping of a human community which can express the beauty and friendship of persons, each of whom is called to 'image' God in devotion to truth, beauty and goodness.

This is not an other-worldly religion. It celebrates the goodness of food and wine, family and society, the beauty of nature and the happiness of using human capacities for discovering truth and making the natural world fruitful.

The Jewish tradition is keenly aware of human 'sin' — of the fact that humans destroy nature and each other in the search for power and pleasure. It points out that such conduct leads to despair, futility and death, which is the judgment of God on evil. But it also holds that each person has an inner capacity for goodness, and that no one is beyond the possibility of forgiveness, for God will never wholly abandon anyone.

The gift of Judaism to the world has been the sense that human morality is of ultimate importance, and that no area of human life is beyond moral scrutiny. It has been the belief that no human situation, even in the darkest times, is beyond hope, if only for a future one cannot see. It has been a commitment to understanding and caring for the world as God's creation, and therefore as a work of wisdom and intellectual beauty.

These are great human goods. Jews have been grievously and unjustly persecuted throughout history, but they have kept an intellectual curiosity and moral drive that has led them to eminence in many areas of human activity. The world would be poorer without them, and even the most secular Jew would admit that Jews would not have remained in existence if it had not been for their religion.

There are many things about Jewish religion that irritate a great many non-religious Jews. But one overwhelmingly good thing is the fundamental belief that this world is good and beautiful, and intellectually fascinating and awe-inspiring. Not all Jews are religious by any means. But there are few Jews who would not, however grudgingly, say that it is belief in the God of Abraham that has made Jews the meticulously scrupulous, intellectually voracious, morally serious, endlessly argumentative, obsessively hard-working, deeply charitable people they are. When all is said and done, that has to be good.

(b) Christianity

Christianity sprang from Judaism, and its distinctive insight is that the creator of all things entered fully into the human situation of pain and distress in the person of Jesus. In that human life the character of the divine love — bringing healing, reconciliation and care for the dispossessed and forgiveness for those oppressed by a sense of guilt — is exemplified. In and through the life of Jesus God acts to reconcile humanity to the divine life. As the early Christian theologian Athanasius put it, God became human in order that humanity might become divine, and might participate in the divine nature.

For those who believe in the incarnation of God in human life, all human life is made holy by the divine presence. This is the foundation for belief in the sanctity of the human person, and in the sacredness of the material world with which God united the divine being in the deepest possible way. Jesus' life was that of someone who befriended people on the fringes of respectable society, who healed the sick and who ruthlessly criticised religious hypocrisy and legalism. This sets the pattern for all Christian lives, as the disciples of Jesus try to follow his example. Most importantly of all for Christians, Jesus was raised from the dead, showing that love is stronger than death and that God wills for all human beings a fulfilment for their lives that cannot be defeated by suffering and pain. This world remains crucially important, for God created it, loves it and wills to redeem it. But the tragedies of this world cannot defeat the purposes of God, and in the resurrection life, joy and love, wisdom and friendship, are promised to all who accept the self-giving love of God.

It is hard to imagine a more positive, world-affirming and morally inspiring vision than this. Christians have founded hospitals, hospices, schools and universities. They have sponsored great works of painting, sculpture, literature and music. Giotto, Rembrandt, Michelangelo, Dante, Augustine, Milton, Palestrina, J. S. Bach, Mozart — without their religiously inspired creative vision the world would be poorer. It was in

Christian Europe that investigation into the world as the creation of one wise and rational God gave rise to modern science. Copernicus (a lay canon of the church), Kepler, Francis Bacon, Isaac Newton – all were inspired to investigate the natural world because of their belief that it was wisely ordered and accessible to human reason, the image of the reason of the creator. From the Platonism of the Greek theologians to the Aristotelian philosophy of Aquinas, and then onto the great philosophical explorations of the Enlightenment, Christian faith has inspired and encouraged rational enquiry into the nature of the cosmos and of human existence. The eighteenth-century Enlightenment itself, with its call for faith in human reason and its concern for human flourishing and happiness, can plausibly be seen as a recovery of primal Christian belief in the rationality of the world, the unique dignity of human life, and an insistence on the vocation of every individual to realise their God-given potentialities. It was in this context that the critical study of history arose, as Christians began to examine the origins of their faith in a series of particular historical events. And it was in this context that belief in full freedom of conscience and equality before God, and in universal human rights and the ideal of universal participation in government, developed from basic belief in human personhood as created in the image of God – free, rational and responsible.

It would be absurd to say that Christianity was the only cause of these things. Like all things human, it has had its internal struggles and tensions. But it would be even more nonsensical to deny the major role that the Christian religion has played in the formation of modern Europe and its rich cultural heritage.

Of course Christianity is not confined to Europe. It is the most widespread religion in the world, existing in virtually every country. It began in West Asia, and Eastern churches have existed in China, Persia and India from very early times. It is strong and vital in North and South America, in Africa, in Russia, in Korea and in many parts of East Asia. It is no longer dominated by Europe, and is taking many new and very diverse cultural forms. In a world that still, in the twenty-first century, is ravaged by famine and violent conflict, the Christian faith, in many indigenous forms, sponsors relief and hospital work, movements for reconciliation such as the Truth and Reconciliation Commission of South Africa, and educational programmes for raising social awareness and creating greater opportunities to participate in political life. It would be wilful blindness to overlook the part Christianity has played throughout the world in helping to raise medical, educational and agricultural standards. It may not always have been an unmixed blessing, allied as it sometimes was with imperial political ambitions. But it has nevertheless been a tremendous influence for good. Things may be bad; but without the Truth and Reconciliation Commission, the Red Cross, the Corrymeela Community, L'Arche and innumerable faith groups working throughout the world, they would undoubtedly be much worse.

(c) Islam

The third great Abrahamic faith is Islam. Muslims founded great hospitals and universities, carried on the traditions of philosophical and scientific enquiry they inherited from Greece and the Byzantine empire, and created a great and sophisticated artistic culture in what Europeans tend to call 'the Dark Ages'. Like Christianity, Islam has in part been compromised by its association with aggressive and imperial ambitions. But it has also helped to modify such ambitions, and to insist ultimately on obedience to a higher law of justice and mercy. Islam gave rise to one of the greatest mystical movements the world has known, and Sufism is still a form of religious practice that seeks a sense of personal unity with the one supreme reality of God rather than just external obedience to religious laws.

Islam rejects the Christian doctrines of the incarnation, the atonement and the Trinity. In that respect it is, I have suggested, rather like unitarianism, upholding belief in one creator God of compassion and mercy, who will hold all people accountable for their deeds. It has the same virtues as Judaism, except that its religious law is meant for all people who will accept it. On the world stage, as a missionary faith it competes with Christianity, and so the possibility of conflict, misunderstanding and intolerance is always present. But it is an over-simplification to suggest that there is bound to be a 'clash of civilisations', as Samuel Huntington suggested in *The Clash of Civilisations*[1]. We need to remember that there are many forms of both Christianity and Islam. Egyptian Copts are not very similar to Southern Baptists; my Muslim friends and colleagues in Oxford are not very like Saudi Arabian *Wahhabis*. In both cases, more exclusive believers say that people other than themselves are not 'really' Christian or Muslim. But such believers are a minority within their own faiths, whether they like it or not. There are lines of division between people, but those lines are cultural, ethnic and linguistic as much as they are religious. And there is good reason to think that a serious and intelligent commitment to a religious tradition will blur the lines of religious division rather than exacerbate them.

I am a Christian, and I am not prepared to renounce belief in the incarnation of God in Jesus, in the efficacy of his atoning death for humanity, and in the Trinitarian reality of God. But I can understand why many religiously devout people cannot accept these beliefs – in the case of Islam, because Muslims feel that associating humanity with God impugns divine sovereignty and absolute 'otherness', that divine justice requires that each person must be held responsible for their own good and bad deeds, and that we must avoid all suspicion of polytheism in our worship of the one and only creator God.

Of course I would put these things differently: God can, precisely because God is sovereign, raise humanity to share in the divine nature. Humans can never overcome their tendency to evil by their own strength. And God can be truly one, while existing in a threefold way, as transcendent, embodied in time and active within all creation, for example. Nevertheless, I accept that there is a core of inescapable disagreement here, which partly goes back to differing views of revelation – in a person, Jesus the Christ, or in a book, the Qur'an. We cannot resolve those differences, and we must follow where our own consciences lead.

What is important is that I, as a Christian, do not caricature Islam as a heresy that wilfully rejects the true God and the true revelation. I must learn to see it, as in fact I see unitarianism, as a path to God that is honestly and reasonably chosen (even though I think it is mistaken). More than that, I can learn to respect the motives of Muslims in wishing to hold true to the absolute transcendence and unity of God, rather than blaming them for rejecting the truth.

Muslims can do the same from their side, learning that Christians are not idolators who replace worship of God with worship of a human person, they are not people who deny human moral responsibility, and they are not polytheists who believe in three Gods. Muslims can learn to respect the Christian claim that the unity of divinity and humanity is closer than that of a wholly other transcendent God to finite creatures, and that a proper sort of sharing in the divine nature (2 Peter 1:4) is possible for humans.

This is what is needed to prevent religious conflict in the modern world. We must affirm our own beliefs with total commitment, but with due humility about how much of it we really understand, in all its diversity and profundity. We must fully accept the right of others conscientiously to disagree, and to manifest their disagreement in practice. And we must try to understand the highest motives that lead others to take other spiritual paths than ours.

There will still remain beliefs and practices that we really do wish to oppose, both within our own religion and in the religions of others. Speaking for myself, the treatment of women as inferior would be one of the practices I would wish to oppose, whether it is Christians or Muslims who do it. But overall there is plenty of room for common social action in mercy and hospitality and kindness between Christians and Muslims, and it is imperative that such commonalities are promoted.

Samuel Huntington says that the major world religions have many key values in common, and recommends, in what he calls the 'commonalities rule', that people should search for and attempt to expand those values that they have in common with other civilisations. The document *Toward a Global Ethic*, drafted by Hans Küng for the 1993 Parliament of World Religions[2] and signed by representatives of all world religions present, is an attempt to spell out some of those commonalities. Commitment to four key issues is noted: to a culture of non-violence and respect for human life; to a just economic order; to tolerance and truthfulness; and to equal rights and partnership between men and women. That, it seems to me, is a strong basis for cooperation between religions, in a new world in which many diverse faiths must live together in peace and in which they have opportunity to undertake programmes of common ethical action. Only if Christianity and Islam, as the two dominant world religions, do this at the highest level – and great efforts are being made to ensure it is done – will there be hope of avoiding that disastrous clash of cultures that would result from a polarisation of stereotyped and mutually hostile images of the 'other'. Religion can create such images. But it also has the greatest power to overcome them. Religion may not be unequivocally good. But if it is dangerous at times, that is far outweighed by the fact that it is one of the last great hopes the world has for peace and a positive future.

(d) Indian traditions

In the global pattern of world religions, Indian traditions play an important part. Central to those traditions is the idea that all reality is included in one supreme absolute, *Brahman*, which has the nature of intelligence and bliss. God is not conceived as a being separate from the universe and in external relationship to it. Rather, the true nature of all real things is that they are parts of a Supreme Self or Spirit. The great Indian theologian Ramanuja held that the universe is the 'body of the Lord', meaning that all things are the expression of Supreme Spirit, which is their inner reality. A rather different tradition is that of Sankara, who held that the whole universe, which appears to be made up of separate things and selves, is in fact just one seamless reality, the Self of all.

For these traditions, the spiritual path is a way of realising that you are part of Supreme Reality; that you are, if you like, divine. But of course you are only a tiny part, or even an illusory appearance, of divinity. You are not omniscient and omnipotent. Nevertheless, when you realise that your true self is identical with the one Self of all, then egoism and self-interest disappear, and you can contemplate all things as parts of the divine. Absolute distinctions between yourself and others fade away, and the whole world can be seen as a set of appearances of one divine reality.

This view seems very different from the Abrahamic vision. It is a form of what Western philosophers call idealism, the theory that everything that seems to be material is actually mind, and part of one supreme mind. But it shares with the Abrahamic view the belief that there is just one Supreme Self, the source of all that exists, and that the goal of human life is to achieve complete knowledge of or union with this Self.

The positive benefit of such views is that they are very inclusive. All things are parts of the divine, and many paths to realising union with the divine are acceptable. There are many gods and goddesses in India, but the major theologians teach that they are all aspects of the one Supreme Self, different ones appealing to different sorts of people. Reverence for images and pictures of the gods is not idolatry, for through them the devotee sees the one Supreme Reality that exists in and through all things.

Humans are not seen as miserable sinners, filled with guilt and destined for hell. Humans are, it is true, bound to a world of suffering and they are ignorant of their true natures, wrongly thinking that they are separate selves and becoming attached to ultimately unsatisfying desires and goals. But by meditation and self-discipline, or by devotion to a spiritual teacher or an enlightened soul (or perhaps to a specific physical appearance of the divine, like Krishna), people can achieve release from suffering and ignorance, and realise that their innermost selves are identical with the one Self of all. This is a very positive view of human life and destiny.

The doctrine of reincarnation or rebirth is part of most Indian religious views, and it seems very different from Abrahamic belief in the resurrection of the body. It *is* different. There is no point in pretending that all religious views are the same. Yet even here we can find commonalities, and aspects of the Indian view that may provide real insight into questions about human destiny.

The commonality is a concern that beyond this life there are rewards and punishments for what we have done. What binds us to suffering is our ignorance of the existence of one Supreme Spirit and our attachment to selfish desires. The religious path is one of overcoming attachment and coming to awareness of the Supreme Self. The doctrine of rebirth is a way of saying that we can go on learning and growing after this life, until at last we overcome the sense of an egoistic self, and are completely absorbed in the one Supreme Self. That is the ultimate human goal.

The emphasis on the divine presence within everyone, in 'the cave of the heart'; on seeing human existence as part of a journey of ever-growing knowledge and compassion; and on seeing all things as existing within God, the one and only self-existent reality of supreme wisdom and bliss – these are all positive beliefs whose acceptance would be expected to increase human wisdom, happiness and compassion. As in all things human, there are negative aspects too, and many cannot accept that these beliefs are actually true. But if the question is about whether religious beliefs are dangerous or helpful to human well-being, there can be little doubt that beliefs like these, if sincerely accepted and acted upon, will produce lives of greater wisdom and compassion. In that sense, even if our own beliefs are very different, we may say that the central beliefs of the major Indian traditions contribute substantially to human good.

(e) Buddhism

The last case I shall consider is East Asian Buddhism. In this set of very various traditions, a creator God is not spoken of. The 'four noble truths' of the Buddha, the Enlightened One, are that everything in this worldly existence involves suffering; suffering is caused by selfish desire; there is a way to release from suffering; and that way is the Eightfold Path. This is a path of moral purity and mental discipline or meditation, leading to the overcoming of attachment to the world. In meditation, the attainment of four mental states is especially important. These are *upekkha* or equanimity (the equal acceptance of joy and suffering alike); *karuna*, compassion for all sentient beings; *mudita*, happiness in the joy of others; and *metta*, universal lovingkindness. The final overcoming of the sense of the egoistic self is liberation, and one who is liberated, said the Buddha, 'has and holds to nothing... is strong in patience... without anger... not stained by worldly pursuit...deep in wisdom, intelligent, knowledgeable... immersed in the deathless... emptied of doubt, unattached and cool'[3].

The East Asian form of Buddhism, *Mahayana*, teaches universal compassion for all beings, and its ideal is the *Bodhisattva*, one who defers personal liberation in order to help beings who are still lost in desire and attachment. Final liberation, *nirvana*, is never described in any literal way, but in entering *nirvana* it is said that a person enters into the deathless, into perfect wisdom and bliss. That is the ultimate goal, but for most people the aim is to grow in mindfulness and compassion, in order to attain a good rebirth, either on earth or in some other realm of being.

Again putting aside the question of truth, it is hard to think of a set of beliefs that is less likely to be harmful, and is more likely to motivate altruistic behaviour and promote psychological well-being. The state of liberation is one of wholly non-selfish compassion. It exemplifies calm mindfulness, serenity and joy, and cultivates a sense of union with a supra-personal state of supreme compassion and bliss (not construed as a personal God, but still being discernibly spiritual or mind-like and more than human). And it promotes belief in the significance of each human life, as each one moves in its own unique way towards a supremely worthwhile goal, to which all the experiences of life contribute, either positively or negatively (as elements to be incorporated in the deathless or overcome and resolved there).

Differences in religion

All these very different religious traditions have developed the idea of one being or state of supreme perfection, and of ways of becoming aware of or even of becoming one with that being or state – ways that will overcome egoism and selfish desire, hatred, greed and ignorance, and bring humans to a state of happiness, wisdom and compassion. It takes a special sort of perverseness to call such traditions harmful or dangerous.

Yet it may seem that the differences between religions cause harm, because they lead to conflict. In this respect, it needs to be remembered that religions only exist because human persons are in a state of bondage to hatred, greed and selfishness. As religious beliefs have to inhabit the minds of such persons, those beliefs do not remain magically pure and uncorrupted. They are affected by the corruptions they exist to extirpate. And so the phenomena of intolerance and repression, irrationality and neuroticism, authoritarianism and hatred of outsiders, come to exist to some degree in all religious institutions. Many of the conflicts between religions are not caused by religious beliefs, but by the imperfections or personality defects of religious believers, which infect their religious beliefs and practices.

In any case, religion is not the only or main cause of disagreements and conflicts between human beings. There are apparently irreconcilable differences of opinion in almost every area of human life – in our assessment of other persons, and in all philosophical, historical, ethical, political, legal, artistic and religious matters – in short, in all human affairs. Such disagreement is not peculiar to religion, but it obviously affects religion. Thus on religious questions such as whether there is a personal God, whether people are reincarnated or resurrected, whether the Bible or the Qur'an is revealed by God, whether the biblical account of creation is literally true or metaphorical – on all these questions people can and do differ.

Particularly since the sixteenth century, increasing knowledge of the diversity of religious views, the rise of the natural sciences as paradigms of knowledge, and acceptance of the unverifiable nature of religious claims, has led to a widespread attitude of critical pluralism with regard to these religious questions. Though questions of truth are at stake, diversity of belief is regarded as inevitable and even to some extent salutary, as leading to more cautious and self-critical statements of religious beliefs. It is generally accepted that sincere religious belief cannot be compelled, so there is no reason why these humanly unresolvable disagreements should lead to conflict. The historical evidence is that they do not do so unless other economic or social factors are at work.

On moral questions such as whether contraception or abortion or euthanasia is morally right or wrong, on whether women should have equal rights to men in all respects, or on whether homosexual sex is morally permissible – on all these questions people differ too.

There is a difference between having a reasoned sincere belief and having a correct belief. The most we can ask of people is that their beliefs should be reasoned and sincere. They should not accept beliefs blindly or without question. They should be aware of the main alternatives. And they should be aware that there exist conscientious disagreements, which remain even when people have tried to be as impartial and objective as they can be.

In practice you still have to opt for some belief (either that abortion is permissible in certain circumstances or that it is not). This may bring you into conflict with others. But it is not religion or morality that causes the conflict. It is sincere commitment to some belief that you think is morally important. It is commitment to morality that causes the conflict. But even though morality can cause conflict, no one would say that morality itself is dangerous or harmful. Morality is essential. What is important is to have the right moral opinions. Unfortunately, there is no neutral way of telling what these are.

People who hold one moral view (say, that abortion is wrong) may well say that a conflicting moral view (that abortion is at least sometimes permissible) is harmful. But this is not the same sort of harm as wilfully lying, cheating or murdering for profit. It is not immorality; it is, or can be, conscientious moral disagreement.

Some opposition to religion is in fact opposition to the moral views that are associated with a specific religious institution (very often the Roman Catholic Church, with its distinctive prohibitions of homoeroticism, extra-marital sex, contraception, abortion and euthanasia). Some religious institutions support moral views with which some others disagree. But religion as such, in all its forms, is not committed to those moral views. In fact, many religious institutions – within Christianity, the Methodist Church and the Church of England, for example – often have no 'official' moral views, offering advice but permitting freedom of conscience on many matters where there is conscientious moral disagreement. It is more accurate to say that some religious people have moral views that are disagreed with by others, than to say that religion is morally harmful. Whether or not those views are harmful is a matter of moral opinion, not a matter of fact.

Some degree of conflict, on both religious and moral issues, may be inevitable – it was inevitable in aggressively anti-religious societies like Soviet Russia, and it may be inevitable in strongly Catholic societies like Croatia. In such cases, one religious contribution often is, and always should be, to counsel peaceful resistance, not violence, and persuasion rather than compulsion. There are outstanding cases in recent times of such a contribution – by Mahatma Gandhi, Desmond Tutu, John Paul II, and thousands of lesser known religious activists and martyrs.

Human beings find it hard to live with differences. Religious believers are human, so religious believers can find it hard too. There will be some matters, both moral and religious, on which different protagonists will not be happy to accept disagreement, and will try as hard as they can to get their views generally enforced by law, whether in a more or a less permissive direction. There will be other matters on which plurality will seem acceptable and even inevitable.

These are difficult issues to negotiate, and they are complicated by the fact that human ignorance, greed and hatred are always negative factors in any complex social situation, religious or otherwise. I have no magic formula to resolve such issues, for I do not think there is one. But no one would dream of saying that morality is dangerous, even though moral beliefs will inevitably lead to disagreement, conflict and perplexity. For similar reasons, no one should dream of saying that religion is dangerous just because religious beliefs also lead to disagreement and perplexity, and can lead to conflict.

In fact most religious beliefs call for respect for others, freedom of conscience, and love or compassion. They call for a serious consideration of how human beings ought to live, in a way that can be truly fulfilling and lead to an increase of respect for life, justice and happiness. If disagreement often seems inseparable from such serious consideration, that is no condemnation of the process. It is a great positive good of religion that it keeps alive questions of the significance of human life and of the right way to live. It keeps alive questions of whether there is a supreme human goal, and of how to attain it. And it keeps alive the question of whether there is an absolute standard of truth, beauty and goodness that underlies the ambiguities and conflicts of human life. Plato said that 'the unexamined life is not worth living'. Religious beliefs are proposed answers to the questions that arise from a sustained examination of life. In that sense, religion is certainly one of the things that makes human life worth living.

What religions need to do now

In this chapter I have tried to show how the major religious traditions of the modern world have contributed positively to human good. Religions, like value systems in general, will never be free of potential conflict and actual disagreement. But they seem to be inseparable from human life, and their overall contribution is, I have argued, positive. Like all belief systems, they are in constant change as they take form in diverse cultures and historical contexts. No one who thinks responsibly could be content with saying that the world religions can continue to exist just as they are. There is always need for reform and critical self-examination, and that must take place if religions are to be a positive force for human good.

In the globalised world of this century, religions need to make sure that they are open and responsive to the things that make for true reverence for the Supreme Good and for true human fulfilment. They need to take full account of the moral and scientific advances that have taken place in the world since the sixteenth century. Religions that take this step will be self-critical, recognising the uncertainty of all human knowledge and accepting that criticism is the most secure path to truth. This does not mean that they must give up their central distinctive doctrines; there will always be diverse religious beliefs, and of course believers will have a firm commitment to their centrally revealed or authoritatively defined truths. But even firm practical commitment can be allied with humility, with an admission that there are many things one does not know and many things that are incompletely understood. Self-criticism is openness to learn from others, not a practical hesitancy about one's own deepest commitments.

Religions also need to focus firmly on what might be called the experiential dimension, seeing the heart of faith not just in the acceptance of intellectual dogmas, but also in morally transforming experiences of spiritual reality. The amazing growth of Christian Pentecostal movements in the modern world, which concentrate on personal experience of the divine Spirit, and are usually committed to non-violence and action to relieve poverty or raise political awareness, highlights this focus. It is also important, however, that religious faith should be securely embedded in a coherent and adequate worldview, so that liberative experience and critical reception of the best scientific advances in the modern world should go together. But the distinctive heart of religion is not intellectual speculation or even moral action. It is the cultivation of an apprehension of an objective reality of supreme value; an apprehension that makes the one who sees more like that which is seen, and which can mediate those values more effectively in all the ambiguities of the human world. It is by their success in cultivating such apprehension and transformative power that religions should judge themselves.

Even though religion is not primarily concerned with moral action, any genuine apprehension of God should lead to committed action for the sake of goodness. One major goal of religion in the modern world should be a commitment to promoting human flourishing and, as much as possible, the flourishing of all sentient beings. Many religions have traditional laws or codes of conduct, and it is always possible that obedience to law might take precedence over concern for straightforward human flourishing. Humanism originated in Europe in the Christian thought of scholars such as Erasmus, with the insight that God's incarnation places an infinite value on human life. It is an important religious imperative that all laws and moral rules should be conducive to the flourishing of all human beings, and especially of those who are deprived, by no fault of their own, of the possibility of well-being. Humanism – or, to put it more accurately and more extensively, a concern for the worth of persons and their development – should never be opposed to religion. For most religions see the personal as the ultimate foundation of all reality, therefore it is a religious obligation to contribute to the flourishing of persons.

Genuine respect for persons entails respecting the right of others to make their own conscientious decisions about ultimate issues, at least where those decisions do not cause obvious and avoidable harm. So each religion in the modern world needs to accept its place as one of many paths to a fulfilling relationship with a supreme spirit. This does not entail vacillation about one's own path, and it does not mean saying that every path is as good as every other. That would be plainly false. What it entails is the acceptance that people do see matters of ultimate value in very different ways, and that there should be no compulsion in matters of religion. If we learn to value the different ways in which people see things, and the different, but genuine, values that they celebrate, that can lead to possibilities of cooperation between faiths, which is one of the most hopeful outlooks for a positive human future.

Can religions take this step to a truly global outlook? In fact, millions of believers already have. Those who hold religion back are those who stick to the view that only their religion provides a set of absolutely certain, unquestionable, definitive and unchanging truths, while everybody else's religion is false. It is that lack of humility, a lack of awareness of the limitations of one's own understanding, and the inability to see or seek the good in the religious beliefs of others, that is harmful.

Some people think that is what all religion is about. But there is another form of religion, whose central core is the overcoming of the egoistic self by a conscious and life-transforming relationship to a spiritual reality of supreme wisdom, creativity, compassion and bliss.

Spiritual reality, however, can be misunderstood, and the right form of a relationship to it can be misconstrued. Religion can be a powerful, destructive force. Believers need to be more aware of this. They need to help their own traditions step forward towards a truly global outlook. We cannot eliminate religions; they are here to stay. It is possible to make them powerful forces for creative living, moral motivation and human reconciliation. It may even be that only reliance on a spiritual power can motivate unlimited love, forgiveness and compassion, or offer hope to a world so lost in hatred and greed. As the philosopher Martin Heidegger said, 'Only a god can save us now.' If that is so, what the world needs is not less religion but more – more of the right kind of religion: self-critical, liberating, humane and tolerant. It is of the greatest importance to investigate, with all the scientific and critical tools at our disposal, how this can best be accomplished.

Despite superficial appearances, religion can be one of the most positive forces for good in human life. In a world where despair, anger and a loss of any sense of human significance are rife, a sense of objective goodness, of human dignity and of cosmic hope is essential for human survival and true well-being. These are things that the world's religious traditions have the potential to give.

There is in my view an overwhelming case for religion, but this has to be a case for discovering and sustaining religious views that protect and promote belief in objective goodness, human flourishing and the moral significance of personal life. Because of the rapid growth of human communications, cultural exchange and scientific knowledge, we are uniquely well placed to move towards a more informed and sensitive approach to such a goal. It is therefore of crucial importance to combine all the resources of science and the traditional wisdom of the world's religions to generate a better understanding of what religion is, at its best, and to devise ways of making that 'best' more evident and attainable.

So is religion dangerous? Sometimes it is. But it is also one of the most powerful forces in the world for good. The best way of ensuring that religion is a force for good is for people of good will and intellectual wisdom to play their part in supporting and shaping it – if, that is, they have initial sympathy with some particular form of its basic presumption that there exists a supreme objective reality and value in conscious relation to which humans can find fulfilment. If they support this, they will of course to some extent spoil it by taking all their own ambiguities and prejudices into it. But at the very least faith can mitigate those shortcomings. At best, religion, the search for supreme goodness, a life lived for the sake of good alone, will help to promote the welfare of all sentient beings. Some danger is unavoidable in any human enterprise. But religion is a main driving force for wisdom and compassion in a world that would be bleak and cruel without it. Religion, to paraphrase Karl Marx, is the compassionate heart of what might otherwise seem to be a cold and heartless world.

Notes

Introduction
1. E. Evans-Pritchard, *Theories of Primitive Religion*, Oxford, Clarendon Press, 1965.
2. Daniel Dennett, *Breaking the Spell*, London, Allen Lane, 2006.
3. James Frazer, *The Golden Bough*, New York, Macmillan, 1992.

Chapter 2
1. For statements of the Second Vatican Council, see the Declaration on Religious Liberty, Declaration on the Relation of the Church to Non-Christian Religions, and Pastoral Constitution on the Church in the Modern World, in *Documents of Vatican Council II*, ed. Austin Flannery, Dublin, Dominican Publications, 1992.

Chapter 3
1. Sayyid Qutb, *Milestones on the Road*, 1965, published in 2006 in English by Maktabah Publishers.
2. UN Commissioner for Refugees, *The State of the World's Refugees: Human Displacement in the New Millennium*, 2006.
3. International Institute for Strategic Studies: The World Military Balance, 2006.
4. David Martin, *Does Christianity Cause War?* Oxford, Clarendon, 2002.

Chapter 8
1. Isaiah Berlin, 'Two Concepts of Liberty', reprinted in *Liberty*, Oxford, Clarendon Press, 2002.
2. T. H. Green, *Lectures on the Principles of Political Obligation*, ed. Paul Harris and John Morrow, Cambridge University Press, 1986.
3. Declaration on Religious Liberty in *Documents of Vatican II* (see above), p. 806.

Chapter 9
1. David Myers, *The Science of Subjective Well-Being*, Guildford Press, 2007. This contains full references to the surveys quoted in the text on well-being and altruism.

2. Harold Koenig, Michael McCullough and David Larson, *Handbook of Religion and Health*, Oxford University Press, 2000.

3. John Nurser, *For All Peoples and All Nations*, World Council of Churches, 2005.

4. European Values Study, Tilburg University, Netherlands – available on the internet.

5. Bernard Spilka et al., *The Psychology of Religion*, Guildford Press, 2003.

6. Michael Argyle, *Psychology and Religion*, Taylor and Francis, 1999.

7. Michael Argyle, *Religious Behaviour*, Routledge, 1958. This contains full references to surveys quoted in the text on mental health.

8. Richard Gregory et al. eds., *Oxford Companion to the Mind*, Oxford University Press, 1987.

9. Farr and Howe, *American Journal of Psychiatry*, 1932.

10. Fleck, *Archiv. Psychiat. Nerven.*, 1935.

11. Ogata and Myakawa, *Psychiatry and Clinical Neurosciences*, 1998.

12. W. Penfield and H. Jaspers, *Epilepsy and the Functional Anatomy of the Human Brain*, London, Churchill, 1954.

13. David Tucker, Robert Novelli and Preston Walker, *Journal of Nervous and Mental Disease*, 1987.

14. W. Oates, *Journal for Pastoral Care*, 1949.

15. H. J. Cronin, *Medical Review*, 1934.

16. Michael Argyle, *Religious Behaviour* (see above).

17. A. Sims, *British Journal of Psychiatry*, 1994.

18. Francis Crick, *The Astonishing Hypothesis*, Simon and Schuster, 1994.

19. Malcolm Jeeves, *Human Nature*, Philadelphia, Templeton Foundation Press, 1996.

20. Malcolm Jeeves (ed.), *From Cells to Souls – and Beyond*, Eerdmans, 2004.

21. G. Edelman, *Bright Air, Brilliant Fire*, Penguin, 1992.

Chapter 10

1. Samuel Huntington, *The Clash of Civilisations*, Simon and Schuster, 1997.

2. Hans Küng, *Towards a Global Ethic*, London, SCM Press, 1998.

3. Discourse 98 in *Discourses of Gotama Buddha*, Middle Collection, trans. David Evans, Janus, 1992.

Index